Customer Acquisition Strategies

Modern Lessons from Ancient Rome's Greatest Entrepreneurs

by Robert C. Lerner

First Edition

Multi-Media Publications Inc.

Oshawa, Ontario

Customer Acquisition Strategies:
Modern Lessons from Ancient Rome's Greatest Entrepreneurs

by Robert C. Lerner

Managing Editor:	Kevin Aguanno
Series Editor:	Mark Kozak-Holland
Copy Editor:	Susan Andres
Typesetting:	Peggy Letrent & Carolyn Prior
Cover Design:	Robert Lerner
eBook Conversion:	Michelina Aguanno

Published by:
Multi-Media Publications Inc.
Box 58043, Rosslynn RPO, Oshawa, ON, Canada, L1J 8L6.
http://www.mmpubs.com/

Lower cover photo courtesy of Shutterstock.

Paperback	ISBN-13: 978-1-55489-175-7
eBook Formats	ISBN-13: 978-1-55489-176-4

Published in Canada. Printed simultaneously in Canada, the United States of America, Australia and the United Kingdom.

CIP data available from the publisher.

Table of Contents

Customer Aquisition Strategies

Acknowledgments

My interest in the ancient Romans' business management techniques has consumed the better part of a decade and, now with this work, resulted in three management texts as part of the *Lessons from History* series. I very much want to thank Kevin Aguanno, Mark Kozak-Holland, and the staff of Multi-Media Publications, Inc. for their continuing support of my efforts to bring the ancient Romans' business insights to modern readers.

I am again deeply indebted to Professor Jacqueline Carlon for her guidance on the Roman history elements critical to constructing this text, her detailed review of this book, and most important, her suggestion that Eumachia be included in this work. I also appreciate the critical comments and suggestions from Dr. Mark Zupan, Ehsan Moghimi, and Shelli Mehri. Of course, any errors or misinterpretations of the sources, whether ancient or modern, are solely my responsibility. Last, I would like to thank my wife for her patience with the time I consumed in completing this project and her assistance in photographing key historical sites in Rome.

Introduction

Along Came the Widow Bates

This text examines customer acquisition methods used in ancient Rome—through inscriptions, tombs, buildings, statuary, containers for transport and sale, mosaics, and ancient texts—and extrapolates those ancient methods into twenty-nine lessons for today. This thematic approach's genesis came from a modern epitaph, at least compared to those of ancient Rome, that I accidentally unearthed during my search for business-related data contained in ancient Roman inscriptions.

This epitaph, one of several variations, is supposedly found on a tomb in Lincoln, Maine. Real or not, the inscription triggered a creative direction, resulting in the writing of this book. The epitaph is as follows:

> *Sacred to the memory of*
> *Mr Jared Bates*
> *who Died Aug. the 6th 1800.*
> *His Widow aged 24*
> *Who mourns as one who can be comforted*
> *lives at 7 Elm Street this village*
> *and possesses every qualification*
> *for a good wife.*[1]

Customer Acquisition

You might ask what direction this is for a business book. The answer is that the Widow Bates' advertising for a new husband on her **deceased husband's tomb** would have made her a good Madison Avenue advertising executive. The widow's creative use of her husband's tomb catalyzed my interest in ancient Roman entrepreneurs' tombs and their marketing efforts as a potential source of modern **customer acquisition** lessons.

Over time, I expanded this study to include many forms of communication the Romans used to market their products and themselves, in life and in death. But before we follow too quickly along the path illuminated by the Widow Bates' acquisition efforts, let's first quickly review how consumers buy, using the traditional Five-Stage Model of the buying process,[2] and then examine the seller's parallel, three-stage customer acquisition process.[3]

The Five-Stage Model of Consumer Buying

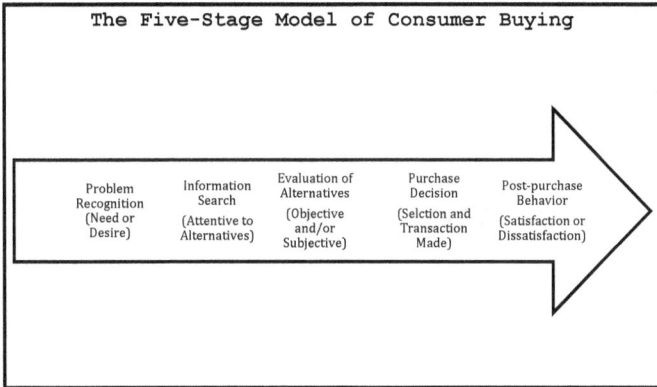

The Five-Stage Model of Consumer Buying

Problem Recognition (Need or Desire)	Information Search (Attentive to Alternatives)	Evaluation of Alternatives (Objective and/or Subjective)	Purchase Decision (Selection and Transaction Made)	Post-purchase Behavior (Satisfaction or Dissatisfaction)

Figure 1.1. Summary of the five stages of the consumer buying decision model.[4] At times, consumers might not follow all the steps or even the chronological sequence of events.[5]

The Five-Stage Model of the buying decision process,[6] shown in Figure 1.1, is initiated when the consumer becomes aware of a problem or a need (Stage 1). That need might be prompted by an internal stimulus (for example, thirst or hunger) or an external stimulus (for example, a friend's new iPhone or an advertisement for an automobile). In Stage 2, "[t]he aroused consumer will be inclined to search for more information,"[7] and in Stage 3, the buyer will evaluate the attributes of the known alternatives (for example, availability, technical specifications, quality, price) to determine which alternative best satisfies the need or desire. The buyer will then (hopefully) execute the purchase (Stage 4) and, if sufficiently satisfied, continue to buy as needed (Stage 5).

Three-Stage Model of Customer Acquisition

The seller's three-stage customer acquisition process (Figure 1.2) parallels the process shown in Figure 1.1. The three stages of customer acquisition and the ancient entrepreneurial role models aligned with each are depicted in Figure 1.2.

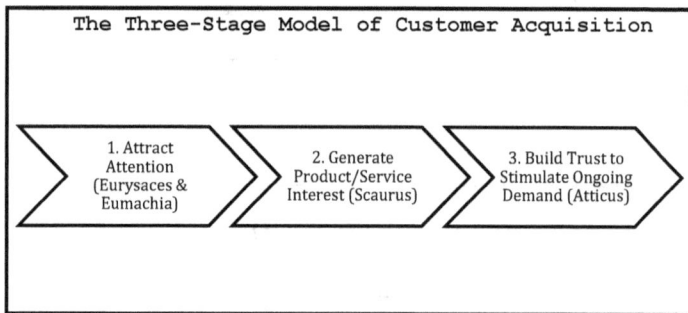

Figure 1.2. Summary of the three stages of customer acquisition (CA) from the seller's perspective and the ancient entrepreneur or entrepreneurs whose marketing activities align with that stage.

Customer acquisition begins with the seller's attempt to exploit a consumer's need or desire:

Stage 1. The initial stage of customer acquisition begins with gaining the attention of potential customers, typically through advertising and marketing programs. (The efforts of our first two entrepreneurs, Eurysaces and Eumachia, will be studied to establish the Stage 1 communication required to reach large audiences.)

Stage 1 is followed by a seller's efforts to inform the consumer about the details of the product or service offered to influence and satisfy the consumer's product search and evaluation criteria:

> **Stage 2. The second stage of customer acquisition involves following up with viewers whose interests have been piqued by the Stage 1 programs in a fashion that educates those potential buyers about the product or service specifications.** (The activities of our third entrepreneur, Scaurus, will illustrate the Stage 2 techniques needed to attract likely buyers.)

The seller's third and final stage of the customer acquisition process is to successfully execute the sale *and* to generate continuing purchases:

> **Stage 3. This final stage's intent is to establish enough trust with potential purchasers that financial transactions (the exchange of goods or services for money) can be conducted repeatedly and expanded over time.**[8] (The actions of Atticus, our fourth entrepreneur, will demonstrate the Stage 3 commitments required from the seller.)

The Four Ancient Entrepreneurs

Eurysaces, whose attention-generating customer acquisition skills are studied in chapters 1 and 2, was an extraordinarily successful baker in the last century before the birth of Christ. Eurysaces, whose full name was Marcus Vergilius Eurysaces, like the Widow Bates, left his marks on the history pages only through his tomb and its engravings, which are still visible in Rome. From Eurysaces, we will establish ten lessons focused on attracting attention in the marketplace.

In chapter 3, Eumachia and her marketing efforts will be analyzed. Eumachia was a wealthy widow thought to have conducted her business late in the last century before the birth of Christ, with significant business interests in sheepherding, the woolen trade, and wine. Eumachia left us a multipurpose commercial building in Pompeii's Forum (marketplace) and a tomb (both badly damaged by Mt. Vesuvius' eruption in 79 AD).

The third entrepreneur whose customer acquisition techniques will be examined in chapter 4 is Aulus Umbricius Scaurus, a fish sauce maker who, like Eumachia, ran his business in Pompeii, but he did so in the decades just before Mt. Vesuvius destroyed the city.[9] Scaurus also left us a tomb to study and mosaics found in his Pompeian home and preserved for centuries under Mt. Vesuvius' ashes, but the most critical information on his business activities is obtained from inscriptions on the shipping containers (*amphorae*) that he used to distribute his products. The five lessons we learn from Scaurus focus on generating interest in one's products or services offered.

In chapter 5, we will study the efforts of the final member of our quartet of ancient entrepreneurs—a man named Titus Pomponius Atticus (called simply Atticus in this text). Atticus, born in 109 BC, was an ancient financier who managed to establish relationships with the political heavyweights of his day, including Julius Caesar, Mark Antony (Caesar's deputy), Cicero (a vehement political opponent of both Caesar and Antony), and Marcus Brutus (one of Caesar's assassins). The five customer acquisition lessons we extract from Atticus' business methods focus on establishing a trusted customer relationship to create repeat demand.

Limitations of Ancient Business Sources

These four entrepreneurs, despite the somewhat limited record of their business activities, still offer a unique opportunity for modern business students to study ancient customer acquisition efforts and to extrapolate those efforts forward into the modern era. There might have been other successful entrepreneurs, but these four people, despite facing great challenges, managed to leave indelible traces of their business interests that have survived for more than two millennia.

The Elite and the Vulgarity of Work

Let's also take a moment to understand the cultural environment of work in which ancient business owners operated. The Roman elite (typically of the senatorial class) viewed businesspersons as lacking dignity and often servile. For an aristocrat, the most acceptable path to power, influence, and wealth was to be descended from distinguished ancestors (Caesar, as many aristocrats, claimed lineage that went back to the gods themselves—Figure 1.3),[10] and then to achieve military conquest and high elective office.

Figure 1.3. The goddess Venus (left), from whom Julius Caesar claimed descent, on a coin produced by a military mint traveling with Caesar in 46/45 BC. The coin also depicts defeated Gallic captives (right). Image courtesy of Classic Numismatic Group, Inc./www.cngcoins.com.

Atticus' close friend and confidant Cicero (Figure 1.4) was one of Rome's most talented politicians. Cicero was also an orator, author, and attorney who rose to the apex of power in the late Roman Republic on the strength of his genius, rather than on his family's history or wealth from great estates. Despite his many achievements, many old aristocratic families regarded Cicero as a mere "new man" lacking the proper bloodlines. If one of the greatest men of his generation (and perhaps in Rome's history) endured such abuse, what could an ordinary businessperson expect?

Figure 1.4. A bust of Marcus Tullius Cicero.[11] Cicero, derided by Rome's aristocrats as a "new man" for he was the first of his family to enter the Senate and rarer still, in the late Republic, to be elected Consul of Rome, the state's highest office. Cicero, despite his unexceptional family background, or perhaps because of it, dismissed most businesspersons as vulgar. However, when Cicero needed political support, he was quick to encourage each tradesman to "preserve intact his workshop where he daily pursues his trade and wins his livelihood, his couch and his bed, in short, the peaceful tenour of his life."[12]

Cicero himself answers this question for us and tells us his opinion (and the opinion of the elite in general) in his book *On Duties*, where he writes, "Unbecoming to a gentlemen . . . and vulgar are the means of livelihood of all hired workmen whom we pay for mere manual labor. . . ."[13]

Even the Emperor Augustus (Figure 1.5) was not immune to similar taunts in his youth. Augustus was accused of having a grandfather who kept a bakery and a mother whose ". . . meal came from a vulgar bakeshop . . . ."[14]

Figure 1.5. A bust of the Emperor Augustus who endured taunts in his youth for supposedly being descended from a mere bakeshop owner.[15]

The aristocratic distaste of the working class, regardless of their wealth or success, meant that Rome's most influential citizens and politicians derided the business efforts of ancient Roman entrepreneurs.

Freedmen and Slaves

At the other end of the spectrum from the Roman
elite's dismissive approach to work were the poor—
they required money to buy food, and so, they needed
work. (See Figure 1.6 for ancient Rome's social
stratification during Emperor Augustus' reign). So,
we must next ask, what hope could a free or slave
laborer, who earned food by the sweat of his or her
brow, have to gain respect in such a class-conscious,
hierarchical society? The simple answer is little or
none.

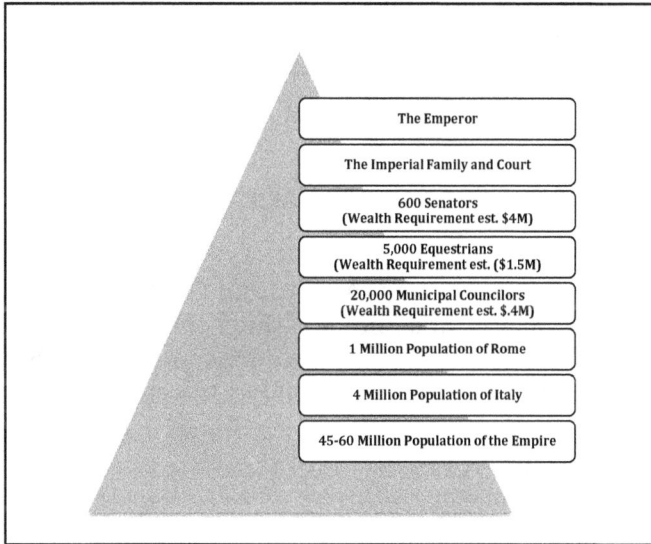

*Figure 1.6. Rome's social stratification and the wealth
requirements of the elite (in current US dollars) during the early
Imperial Age under Emperor Augustus (about the time of Jesus'
birth).[16]*

Slaves, regarded under the law as mere property,
possessed no rights and had no status, but they

were still valued based on their physical attributes, skills, country of origin, and *occupation*, so a cook or tutor had greater value than a farmhand did.[17] Thus, an occupational title at least provided a slave with a form of value/identity in Roman society. This desire for identification carried forward to the ex-slave (*freedman*). Ex-slaves, unlike slaves, had limited rights of citizenship, but they were never accepted as anything other than what today might be dismissed as low class, despite any wealth they might possess. This was still an improvement from their former status as a slave, and a male child of a freedman in Rome obtained all freeborn citizen rights. However, that child still potentially endured the discrimination of his descent, which could limit upward mobility.

Work as a Means of Establishing Identity

Work, therefore, for both slaves and freedmen, offered a means of demonstrating some importance within societal structures that depended so much on genealogy. Sandra R. Joshel in her study of occupational inscriptions, *Work, Identity and Legal Status at Rome*, reports that, "Lacking a heritage, socially acknowledged kin, a place in the social order, even names of their own, slaves did have their work . . . In this light, slaves' use of occupational title (*on funerary monuments*) stems from the poverty of their social position."[18] Joshel states, "The predominance of slaves and ex-slaves among those who identified themselves as the producers of goods and services (*on tombs*) seems to bespeak slaves' awareness of the worth of their activities."[19]

The Importance of Tombs and Their Epitaphs

Tombs were important for both rich and poor alike, for Romans not only believed that "the spirits of the dead continued, 'to live in, or in the vicinity of, the tomb,'"[20] but also that tombs and their epitaphs were to commemorate (for eternity) one's role in Roman society, whether significant (that is, the wealthy) or marginal (that is, the poor).

Rome's aristocrats "emphasized their public position and achievements rather than their role in the marketplace."[21] The aristocrats' achievements, engraved on their tombs, typically included political offices held, military victories, and acts of munificence. Epitaphs were specifically designed to engage viewers as they passed the tomb hoping they would speak of the deceased because any "stopping and contemplating (of) the tomb prolonged and called forth the memory of the dead."[22]

Some tombs of the rich even included a bench to allow viewers to sit and rest while they read aloud the tomb's message about the deceased aristocrat's life,[23] for ancient Romans did not read silently.[24] Julius Caesar's ability to read silently was unique, and an ancient historian noted it.[25]

An Example of an Upper-Class Funerary Inscription

An example of a typical upper-class Roman's inscription emphasizing position and achievement can be seen on the equestrian Titus Vennonius Aebutianus' tombstone dedicated by his wife:

> *To Titus Vennonius Aebutianus,*
> *Son of Titus, of the Stellarina tribe,*
> *Patron and citizen of the colony of*
> *Augusta Taurinorum,*
> *Roman equestrian with the public*
> *horse, selected as juror in five boards*
> *of jurors, caretaker of the state of*
> *Albenses Pompeiani and of the district of*
> *Laurentum and Lavinium, priest of the*
> *same district, Munia Celerina, daughter*
> *of Quintus, his wife, dedicated this to her*
> *dearest husband.[26]*

(Author's notes: Augusta Torinorum is now modern Torino; the horse was provided at the public's expense; Albenses Pompeiani is modern Alba, Laurentum and Lavinium were ancient cities a few miles southwest of Rome.)

Examples of Non-elite Roman Funerary Inscriptions

For slaves or ex-slaves, a tomb and its epitaph, however simple, provided a unique opportunity not only to commemorate their existence, but also to state their worth in society because funerary monuments were an acceptable means (and perhaps their only means) for the lower classes to "shift attention from birth and honor to productive activities . . . ."[27]

An example of Roman funerary inscription or epitaph by a slave that mentions the deceased's occupation is as follows:

> *To Italia, dressmaker of Cocceia Phyllis,*
> *lived 20 years; Acastus, her fellow slave,*
> *made this because of her*
> *poverty.*[28]

In this example, we find the name (Italia) and age (20 years) of the deceased as well as her occupation (dressmaker), offering the slave societal identification. We also learn from her epitaph that she was so poor that a close friend (Acastus, a fellow slave) paid for her funerary monument because her owner (Cocceia Phyllis) apparently did not care enough to provide the funding.

What follow next are two additional inscriptions, but the occupational references contain more information than just the deceased's occupation; they also provide *a location* for that occupation. The first epitaph is for a former slave who was an ivory worker:

> *Sextus Clodius Amoenus,*
> *freedman of Sextus, worker in ivory*
> *near the temple of Hercules the Firstborn.*[29]

The second epitaph is left by a husband, a former slave of Gaius Julius with a fruit stand near the imperial box at the Circus Maximus on the days when there were no chariot races and the stadium was used as a marketplace, in memory of his wife, a freedwoman:

> *Gaius Julius Epaphra, fruit seller*
> *in the Circus Maximus, in front of the*
> *imperial box, made this for himself and*
> *for Venuleia Helena, freedwoman of*
> *Gnaeus, son of Gnaeus, his wife.*[30]

A third example takes these forms of identification even further and much closer to that of the Widow Bates:

> *Lucius Furius Diomedes, freedman*
> *of Lucius, stone engraver on the Via*
> *Sacra, dedicated this to Cornelia*
> *Tertulla, daughter of Lucius, his wife.*[31]

Diomedes, a surviving spouse and a stone engraver, took the opportunity to include his business address on his wife's tomb (Figure 1.7). Thus, we see the tomb would have been an effective testimony to the quality of Diomedes' engraving skills. As important as what is said in this epitaph is what is absent here—any praise of or information about Diomedes' deceased, freeborn spouse, beyond the presentation of her father's name.

This epitaph carved by her stonemason husband was less about the dearly departed and much more about this widower's ongoing stone-carving business. Diomedes' engraved statement of occupation, enhanced with an address, not only demonstrated his skill and status in society, but also provided a medium for advertising his business.

Figure 1.7. The quality of engraving on Cornelia Tertulla's tomb carved by her stonemason husband. The tomb advertises both the quality workmanship that Diomedes used in service to his deceased wife and the location of his business.[32] A freed slave, Diomedes married his former owner's freeborn daughter, and he was likely set up in business by Lucius Furius, his father-in-law and former owner.

Guidance from Modern CA Experts

We earlier identified the four ancient entrepreneurs who are the primary subjects of this text, and now, I would like to identify the three modern customer acquisition experts I have selected to assist us in determining the effectiveness of the strategies that those entrepreneurs used and the relevance of their CA activities to the modern marketplace.

David Ogilvy

The first expert I will draw on is the acknowledged "King of Madison Avenue," David Ogilvy.[33] As one of the great advertising executives of the twentieth century, Ogilvy's comments will primarily center on Stage 1 (attract attention) and Stage 2 (generate a product/service focus) of the customer acquisition process.

Figure 1.8. David Ogilvy, the founder in 1948 of Ogilvy & Mather, an ad agency that today is one of the world's largest advertising agencies. Photo: Courtesy Everett Collection.

Who better to help us evaluate the attention-generating actions of our four entrepreneurs than the man whom the *New York Times*, after his passing, called "The Father of Soft Sell in Advertising"?[34]

In discussing Ogilvy, the *Times* also noted, "In a career that spanned five decades, Mr. Ogilvy created one of the biggest ad agencies in the world and helped alter the landscape of American advertising."[35] Ogilvy not only led Ogilvy & Mather, one of America's great Madison Avenue ad agencies, he also wrote two bestselling books on advertising, from which we will frequently draw: *Confessions of an Advertising Man* (which has sold more than 1.5 million copies)[36] and *Ogilvy on Advertising*. Perhaps one of the most important points Ogilvy made about his persona was his statement, "If you can't advertise yourself, what hope do you have of being able to advertise anything else?"[37]

Ogilvy successfully advertised himself and, along the way, a plethora of quality products. Additionally, Ogilvy created a particular print ad format still emulated. The "Ogilvy format," as can be seen in the classic Hathaway shirt ad (Figure 1.9), consists of three elements:

1. The product image (most often placed in the ad's most visible portion—the top segment),

2. The headline or tagline sized for immediate visibility, and

3. The informative copy.

The man in the Hathaway shirt

AMERICAN MEN are beginning to realize that it is ridiculous to buy good suits and then spoil the effect by wearing an ordinary, mass-produced shirt. Hence the growing popularity of HATHAWAY shirts, which are in a class by themselves. HATHAWAY shirts wear infinitely longer—a matter of years. They make you look younger and more distinguished, because of the subtle way HATHAWAY cut collars. The whole shirt is tailored more *generously*, and is therefore more *comfortable*. The tails are longer, and stay in your

trousers. The buttons are mother-of-pearl. Even the stitching has an ante-bellum elegance about it.

Above all, HATHAWAY make their shirts of remarkable *fabrics*, collected from the four corners of the earth—Viyella and Aertex from England, woolen taffeta from Scotland, Sea Island cotton from the West Indies, hand-woven madras from India, broadcloth from Manchester, linen batiste from Paris, hand-blocked silks from England, exclusive cottons from the best weavers in America. You will get a

great deal of quiet satisfaction out of wearing shirts which are in such impeccable taste.

HATHAWAY shirts are made by a small company of dedicated craftsmen in the little town of Waterville, Maine. They have been at it, man and boy, for one hundred and fifteen years.

At better stores everywhere, or write C. F. HATHAWAY, Waterville, Maine, for the name of your nearest store. In New York, telephone MU 9-4157. Prices from $5.50 to $25.00.

Figure 1.9. The classic Ogilvy advertising format of image, headline or tagline, and informative copy. Image: Courtesy of Advertising Archive/Courtesy Everett Collection.

Donald Trump

The second modern expert I will use to discuss the CA processes the ancient entrepreneurs used is

Donald Trump. Trump's early business success, which consistently demonstrated his innate ability to consummate big deals, is often overshadowed by his entry into the political arena. However, his dealmaking and his success in creating a powerful brand offer relevant insights into our ancient entrepreneurs' activities.

Much has been written about Donald Trump, including his being called ". . . the most daunting entrepreneur since the Astors, Vanderbilts, and Whitneys . . . ,"[38] but perhaps the best description of the man comes from Trump himself. In the opening paragraph of his first book, *Trump: The Art of the Deal*, published in 1987 when he was just thirty-one, Donald Trump wrote,

"I don't do it for the money. I've got enough, much more than I'll ever need. I do it to do it. Deals are my art form."[39]

Trump, from his opening sentences, announces to the world that he is already rich—very rich—, but his monument to himself and for the world are his deals. They are his "art form," and Trump's ability to repeatedly do the "big deals" is the best testimony we have to his business acumen; deals require both buyers and sellers, and there is still no shortage of candidates looking to "do deals" with "The Donald." Even in his eleventh book, *Think Big,* published in 2007, Trump delivers the same message he has articulated for decades, "I'm still making deals, big deals."[40]

Figure 1.10. The consummate dealmaker, Donald Trump. Photo: Courtesy of Gage Skidmore.[41]

Steve Jobs

Besides Ogilvy and Trump, I have also included an occasional comment by Steve Jobs or advertising examples from his company Apple. Jobs, according to the *New York Times*, "was the visionary co-founder of Apple who helped usher in the era of personal computers and then led a cultural transformation in the way music, movies, and mobile communications were experienced in the digital age."[42] Steve Jobs was only fifty-six when he died on October 5, 2011.

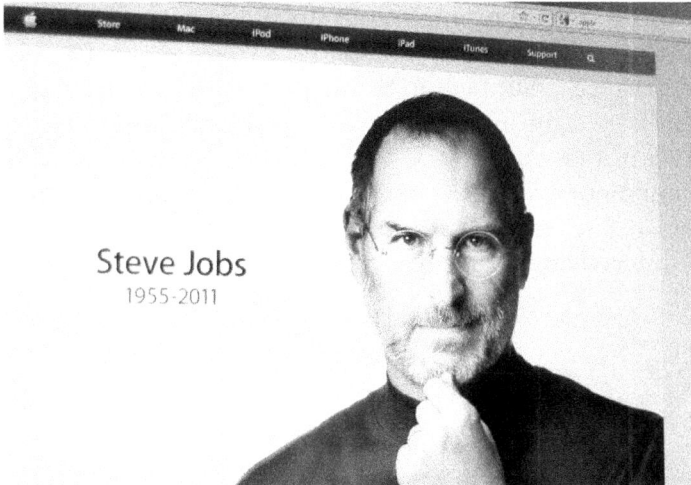

Figure 1.11. Commemorative photo of Steve Jobs posted by Apple on its home page. Steve Jobs passed away on October 5, 2011. Photo: Courtesy of Shutterstock.

According to *Bloomberg,* on September 30, 2013, Apple was the world's most valuable brand, valued at $98.3 Billion.[43]

Timelessness of Skillful Customer Acquisition

The customer acquisition genius of Steve Jobs, Donald Trump, and David Ogilvy helped propel their companies, their brands, and themselves to the top of their chosen markets. Each man was (and still is, in the case of Trump) an excellent promoter of his business interests and himself—you cannot separate one from the other.

The same very much holds true for our four ancient entrepreneurs—you also cannot separate their personal promotion from that of their business interests. Although thousands of years separate Eurysaces, Eumachia, Scaurus, and Atticus from Ogilvy, Trump, and Jobs, the customer acquisition techniques they used in antiquity to attract consumer attention, generate product interest, and stimulate demand can still be discerned in their modern counterparts' actions.

CHAPTER 1

Eurysaces (Part 1)

Bread and Circuses

Bread was a critical staple of life for the ancient Romans, so much so that the Roman poet Juvenal, in the late first century AD, famously wrote, "The people that once used to bestow military commands, high office, legions, everything, now limits itself. It has an obsessive desire for two things only—bread and circuses."[1] Ancient Rome's astute politicians helped feed those desires with spectacular games and a public dole of grain used for baking bread. Rome's impoverished masses were willing to vote for the politicians who helped fill their stomachs.

The Emperor Augustus even commented on the importance of the grain dole: "I was strongly inclined to do away with the distributions of grain (to some 200,000 men of Rome monthly),[2] . . . but I did not carry out my purpose, feeling sure that they would one day be renewed through desire for popular favor."[3] Using bread to buy political support did not end with Augustus' rule (27 BC–AD 14), and it did not begin with him, either. For nearly two centuries, earlier politicians began to use grain to buy popularity. The governmental dole was then formalized in 123 BC to establish control over the practice.[4]

However, in ancient Rome, there were frequent periods of social unrest when supplies of grain were interrupted because of bad harvests, war, and transport bottlenecks, creating shortages in bread's availability or affecting its price.[5] The Emperor Claudius (who ruled the Roman Empire from AD 41–54) was sufficiently concerned with shipping capacity and its impact on grain imports that he offered "special privileges to those (shippers) who built vessels of a minimum capacity of 10,000 modii (about 70 tons) and kept them in services for six years . . . ."[6]

Figure 2.1. Bronze bust of the Emperor Claudius who was very concerned with the unrest that might follow in the wake of grain shortages.[7]

Bread and Jesus

The need for bread to feed the hungry in the ancient
Roman province of Judea can also be found in the
New Testament's Gospel of Mark. Many scholars
think the Gospel of Mark was written between 65
AD and 75 AD (the Emperor Nero reigned from
AD 54–68, and the Emperor Vespasian from AD
69–79).[8] Mark tells of the two miracles of Jesus
feeding his multitude of followers. The first miracle,
The Feeding of the Five Thousand, told in Mark
6:34–44 (the "miracle of the five loaves and two fish")
describes how Jesus fed a crowd of five thousand
from five loaves and two fish.

The second miracle, The Feeding of the Four
Thousand, is recounted in Mark 8:1–10 (the "miracle
of the loaves and fishes"). Jesus again desired to feed
a hungry crowd (the four thousand) with him and
miraculously multiplied seven loaves of bread and a
few fish into a quantity sufficient for the multitude
following in his wake. Before performing this
miracle, however, Jesus first had enquired whether
there was food for the hungry, and his disciples
asked him, "Where can anyone get enough bread
to satisfy them here in this deserted place?"[9] The
absence of bread among Jesus' followers meant that
thousands would go hungry, so divine intervention
was required.

Figure 2.2. A Coptic icon depicts the miracle of Jesus feeding thousands with but seven loaves of bread when his disciples could not procure enough bread for his multitude of followers.[10]

The Business of Bread

By the time of Jesus' ministry, we know that the need for a miracle in a remote Roman province was an exception, and not the rule, for baking enterprises spread across the Roman Empire. In the biblical miracles of the loaves, most likely, bakeries were not proximate, and even if they were, we can assume that there was not enough money to make the purchases for the hungry.[11] The result of either shortage (money to pay or product availability) was that Jesus was required to twice multiply the few available loaves of bread to feed his hungry following.

Jesus' miracles involving the absence of bread and the long history of imperial sensitivity to the availability and price of bread provide strong evidence of the existence of significant business opportunities to supply bread. For when there is either a shortage of product or pricing inequities, the entrepreneur usually steps in quickly, regardless of the century. This can be readily seen with bread in ancient Rome, for by the fourth century AD, there were more than 250 bakeries (Figure 2.3) in Rome itself, "and it is unlikely that the number had been significantly smaller in previous centuries."[12]

Figure 2.3. An example of an ancient bakeshop, this one from a Pompeian fresco.[13] The bread depicted above closely resembles the photo of a carbonized loaf of bread shown in Figure 7.5.

The Renown of Eurysaces the Baker

The story of Eurysaces, an ex-slave,[14] is not miraculous, but a more mundane testament to one man's efforts to make bread available and the sophisticated means he used to communicate his role in Rome's bread business. In the process, Eurysaces, who worked his entrepreneurial miracle just a few decades before Jesus' birth,[15] managed to become wealthy.[16] There might have been other significant bakers before Eurysaces, but we know little or nothing of them.

We also cannot find a nonbiblical character more memorably linked to bread for at least another seventeen centuries, and that person's name is John Montagu (1718–1792). Montagu is much better known by his title, the 3rd Earl of Sandwich, the man for whom the sandwich is named. The Earl was not a baker such as Eurysaces, nor was he a man of the cloth, for the sandwich's creation supposedly happened when the Earl requested a slab of meat be placed between two slices of bread so he could continue to gamble uninterrupted by eating.[17]

You might now ask of Eurysaces' fame—for he is not commonly known outside selected academic circles. In addition, unlike many wealthy and famous men of the Roman Republic and of Imperial Rome, Eurysaces was an ex-slave and, therefore, of low status. Thus, the questioning of such a man's fame is legitimate, and this work intends to justify the importance of this ex-slave in the study of modern customer acquisition practices.

Eurysaces the Ex-Slave

Eurysaces is assumed an ex-slave because, as engraved on his tomb, his full name was Marcus Vergilius Eurysaces. This combination of a Roman name (Marcus Vergilius, likely his former master) and a name of Greek origin (Eurysaces) indicates freedman status, as does his occupation of baking, which was traditionally associated with slaves and ex-slaves.[18]

For many scholars, one additional rationale for Eurysaces' servile background (in a somewhat circular form of reasoning) is the view that Eurysaces' tomb, most of which still stands in Rome, is tasteless (Figure 2.4) and, therefore, must be an ex-slave's product.[19] As we saw earlier, a tomb can be an intriguing vehicle for determining the message or messages Romans wished to provide their contemporaries and posterity.

Figure 2.4. Eurysaces' Tomb, which stands at 36 feet, as seen in Rome today. Some scholars have used the uniqueness of this tomb's design to indicate Eurysaces' freedman status. Photo: Robert Lerner.

Eurysaces' Tomb

Figure 2.4 shows the Tomb of Eurysaces as it stands in Rome today. Eurysaces' mausoleum is no ordinary tomb; we will discuss its complex design characteristics, not the least of which is its size (at nearly three stories tall, it was built on a scale of those built by the wealthiest Roman aristocrats).

By comparison, Figure 2.5 shows the funerary plaque of another, far more ordinary, baker named Adrastus. The simple monument he left to commemorate his life and his work is inscribed with only two words, *Adrastus pistor* (Adrastus baker), and its dimensions are not measured in many stories or tens of feet, but in just a few inches.

Figure 2.5. A photograph of the baker Adrastus' tombstone, perhaps commissioned by Adrastus, his family, his friends, or his guild. This small tombstone is housed in the National Roman Museum (Baths of Diocletian / The Epigraphic Museum). Photo: Robert Lerner.

Given the grand size of Eurysaces' mausoleum, he faced significant construction costs that could only have been borne by one of great wealth. But despite that wealth, Eurysaces' tomb was still designed to emphasize his occupation as a baker. Eurysaces' elephantine efforts to document his occupational status through his tomb is much akin to Adrastus' more traditional and modest effort to draw attention to his status through a simple epitaph on a plain stone slab, but the scale is vastly different.

Fortunately, Eurysaces' tomb has survived the depredations of the passing centuries in good condition, and so, we can study the monument to learn of the man and his genius for customer recruitment and his promotion of his work, himself, and his product—bread.

The Site for Eurysaces' Tomb

Eurysaces' effort to achieve immortality and
perhaps to gain additional customers along the way
began with the funerary monument's placement.
Eurysaces did not choose a typical location suitable
for an ex-slave's tomb; instead, he chose a prime
location—again more appropriate to the elite, for
he "located the tomb on a plot of land between
two main thoroughfares into the city (*of Rome*).
Eurysaces seems to have taken full advantage of the
plot's unique location to draw viewers not just from
one, but two roads, thus potentially doubling his
audience."[20]

Funerary monuments by law were to be outside
the city, but during the Roman Republic, tombs were
typically built on well-established roadways leading
in and out of the city.[21] "Competition existed for
the prime positions visible to travelers, who might
read the inscriptions and reflect on the life and
achievements of the deceased."[22]

The wealthy, just as today, could then obtain
the best construction sites (and the poor could not).
Therefore, we can reasonably assume that the
closer a burial plot was to the city proper, the more
expensive that plot was. Eurysaces seems to have
been determined to maximize the viewing audience's
size and accomplished this by selecting a site for his
mausoleum, not just in a heavily traveled location,
but also one fed by *two* converging roads.

Potential Site Selection Criteria

We can assume Eurysaces applied substantial
forethought and planning to the project (a discussion

of potential lead-times between construction and entombment can be found in chapter 2), based on his careful selection of the real estate on which he intended to build his tomb. The variables Eurysaces and his architect likely discussed would have included site size and availability, site and construction costs, visibility from and proximity to major roads, distance from Rome's center, and the size and placement of adjacent tombs that could possibly obscure his tomb (these five evaluation criteria are shown in Figure 2.6).

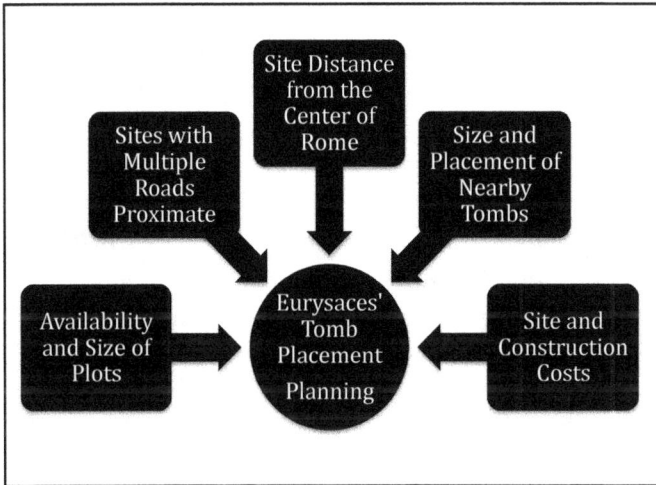

Figure 2.6. The potential evaluation criteria Eurysaces used in selecting his monument's location. These criteria are similar to those businesspeople today consider essential to their construction programs—location, availability, access, adjacent structures, and cost.

From these assumptions about Eurysaces' funerary plot selection and detailed planning efforts carefully aimed at maximizing his viewing audience, we can formulate our first simple but important Stage 1 customer acquisition lesson.

Lesson 1: Plan Thoroughly

Successful CA campaigns are not the result of chance; they start with meticulous planning to ensure the proper identification of the target audience and the method or methods by which the selected audience will be reached. Additionally, thorough planning can often compensate for "bad luck" and helps to create "good luck." David Ogilvy was careful to stress this point when he wrote about developing a product's advertising strategy: "You don't stand a tinker's chance of producing successful advertising unless you start by doing your homework."[23]

A Modern Example of the Value of Planning

An example of perhaps the most effective customer recruitment campaign of the twentieth century was Volkswagen's "Think Small" advertising campaign.[24] This campaign, begun in 1959 by Doyle Dane Bernbach (DDB), demonstrates detailed planning's value. The entire DDB advertising team, after being awarded the Volkswagen contract, traveled to VW headquarters in Germany and spent days talking to employees and touring manufacturing facilities and eventually emerged with a selling proposition—that the VW was an "honest car."[25]

The ad ultimately implemented, although it copied "the traditional look of Ogilvy ads,"[26] was revolutionary in its minimalist approach and successful beyond anyone's expectations, vaulting Volkswagen into the top tier of the world's automobile manufacturers. In this case, research showed that presenting the VW as a small (and honest) car was much more effective than trying to make the car into something it was not.

Think small.

Figure 2.7. Advertising Age selected Volkswagen's Think Small Ad campaign as the greatest print advertising campaign of the twentieth century. Image: Courtesy Advertising Archive/Courtesy Everett Collection.

Thorough Planning Cannot Save a Doomed Product

Even the greatest research and planning will not save a product doomed to failure. Another car ad, this one from the late 1950s, demonstrates this corollary to our above lesson. The ad campaign was for the infamous Ford Edsel, and Figure 2.8 shows a 1958 advertisement for the auto.

Figure 2.8. An early Edsel advertisement—the Edsel was blessed with thorough research, but clearly was not here to stay, for the product failed to meet customer desires. Image: Courtesy Advertising Archive/Courtesy Everett Collection.

Although the Edsel was designed with state-of-the-art motivational research and backed by Ford's advertising might, the car still failed.[27] Possibly, Edsel's sales were hampered by the impact of full-page color advertisements highlighting the stylistically novel vertical front-grill design. "The grill was quickly dubbed the 'horse collar' by many. Others, even less complimentary, said it looked like a toilet seat or, worse, like a part of the female anatomy."[28]

Unfortunately, for Ford, no analysis and planning could save the doomed Edsel, for despite all Ford's sophisticated efforts to identify the customers' desires, the Edsel missed the mark because buyers did not know what they wanted. Steve Jobs of Apple famously noted in 1989, "You can't just ask customers what they want and then try to give that to them. By the time you get it built, they'll want something new."[29]

A Final Caution on Using Customer Research

David Ogilvy, unlike Jobs, firmly believed in customer research but also understood the power of management judgment and cautioned that you should not over depend on research (as in the Edsel's case). Ogilvy's colorful phraseology for this advice was not to use research "as a drunkard uses the lamppost, for support rather than illumination."[30]

Eurysaces' Tomb Design

We saw earlier that Eurysaces did his research and identified a visible site for his tomb. We will next examine the impact and import of that tomb's shape. Eurysaces did not select a circular, square, or rectangular design; instead, he chose a trapezoidal design (and not a uniform trapezoid as in Figures 2.9 and 2.10). Professor Lauren Hackwork Petersen in her text *The Freedman in Roman Art and Art History* argues that the tomb's unique shape was possibly the result of the plot's limited space because of existing tombs and the two roads bounding the plot.[31]

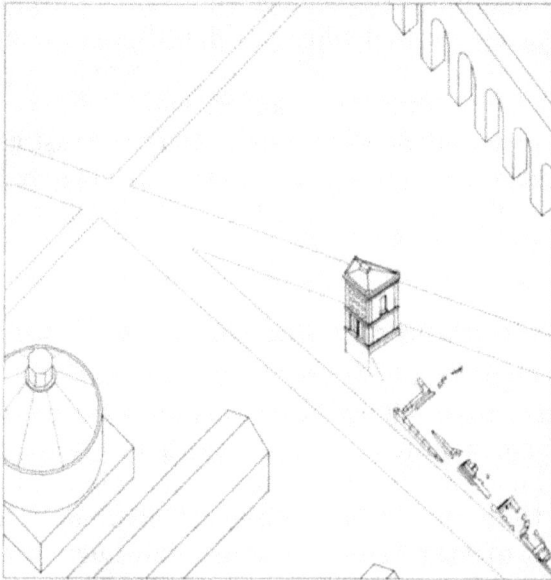

Figure 2.9. The placement of Eurysaces' Tomb relative to the converging roads (Via Praenestina on the north side and Via Labicana on the south) at the time of construction. (Drawing from Robert Coates-Stephens "Porta Maggiore: Monument and Landscape—Archaeology and topography of the southern Esquiline from the Late Republican period to the present" published by L'Erma di Bretschneider, Rome 2004).

Besides eschewing an isosceles trapezoid (equal legs), Eurysaces did not attempt to fit a more traditionally shaped (rectangular) tomb in the space as seen in Figure 2.10. Either of the more traditional shapes would have resulted in additional unused space—likely expensive space. Eurysaces chose to emphasize size and maximize viewer proximity (along the Via Labicana as shown in Figure 2.10), rather than esthetics and symmetry.

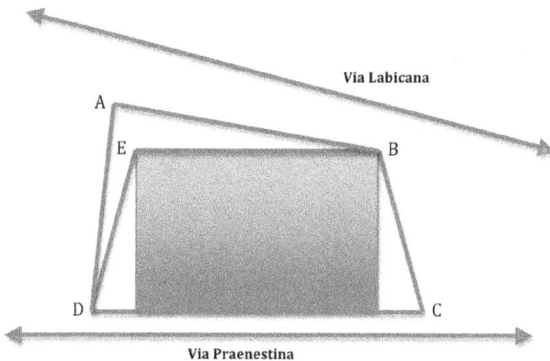

Figure 2.10. If looking from the Via Praenestina, an isosceles trapezoid DEBC, fitting into the oddly shaped trapezoid chosen by Eurysaces (DABC) but with significant lost space (DABE). If a rectangular shape (shaded) had been chosen for placement on the plot, even greater usable (and expensive) space would have been lost.

Eurysaces likely paid a premium for the plot and, similar to most business people today, probably wanted to waste none of that premium real estate for the esthetics of a more traditional structure if it did not fully use the available space purchased. Regardless of the underlying rationale (a desire for a unique design or to maximize all available space), the result was the creation of an extraordinarily different tomb. From Eurysaces' apparent efforts to establish visual separation from other tombs in the area, we have our second CA lesson.

Lesson 2: Seek Separation from the Pack

We cannot know why Eurysaces conceived his design, but we know that the tomb's ungainly shape seems optimally aligned to offer the greatest viewing impact to the passerby. We know this because, as seen in Figure 2.10, the tomb's longest side (at nearly 20 feet) faces the Via Praenestina, thus offering a longer viewing time and the greatest proximity to the tomb for a passerby.

When seeking potential customers' attention, you must identify a means to separate your product or service from your competitors. If you fail to separate, you risk invisibility in the marketplace, which results in little but apathy from a potential buyer. Looking again to David Ogilvy for guidance, we find he has a simple rationale for seeking distinction: "You cannot bore people into buying."[32]

The Greatest TV Commercial of All Time

Perhaps one of the best modern advertisements that reaped the benefit of a willingness to gain distinction and separation from the pack was the "1984" advertisement run by Steve Jobs and Apple to introduce the Macintosh that aired during Super Bowl XVIII on January 22, 1984. The Apple ad, directed by Ridley Scott and available in its entirety on YouTube, was ranked as the #1 TV commercial of all time.

Figure 2.11. An image from Apple's bold "1984" ad aired during the 1984 Super Bowl and ultimately ranked by TV Guide as the greatest TV commercial of all time. Image: Courtesy Advertising Archives.

The ad cleverly proclaimed that the Macintosh, introduced in 1984, would restore freedom to the personal computer marketplace and save the world from the fate depicted in George Orwell's dystopian novel *1984*.[33]

Eurysaces Also Achieves Separation

Eurysaces, despite the limited media available in his time, acquired a highly visible location, selected an ungainly shaped design for his edifice, and then invested the capital required to build his monument to brazenly be "in the face" of every passerby regardless of his or her status. Eurysaces' tomb still evinces awe and engenders discussion more than two thousand years after its construction, showing that Eurysaces had a Steve Jobs-like vision to successfully separate his tomb from the pack.

Supersizing Roman Tombs

Eurysaces the ex-slave not only selected an oddly shaped monument design, but also one nearly 33 feet (3 stories) high and extraordinarily massive (the perimeter is about 54 feet).[34] The two examples that follow demonstrate that large tombs for Rome's elite were just coming into style when Eurysaces constructed his edifice. The first example of a gigantic aristocratic tomb is that of Caecilia Metella, built about 30 BC (Figure 2.12).

This tomb consisted of a circular drum 36 feet tall with a diameter of nearly 100 feet set on a square base measuring almost 100 feet per side. An aristocratic family constructed this tomb—in this case, the descendants of Marcus Crassus, one of the wealthiest senators in Rome's history and a political partner of Julius Caesar. Eurysaces' sizing of his tomb placed him in elite company.

Figure 2.12. An illustration of the tomb of Caecilia Metella, a descendant of one of Rome's wealthiest senators, Marcus Licinius Crassus.[35]

The second example of a grandiose tomb (Figure 2.13) is the pyramid-shaped mausoleum of Gaius Cestius Epulo, a Roman magistrate who seems to have been enamored with the pyramids of Egypt[36] or of ancient Nubia (modern Sudan), where Cestius might have served in a military campaign.[37] Cestius' tomb, built in under a year sometime between 18 BC and 12 BC, stands at more than 120 feet, and it is about 100 feet on a side.

Figure 2.13. Gaius Cestius Epulo's tomb built between 18 BC and 12 BC. The tomb's inscription states that construction was begun after Cestius' death and was completed in just 330 days.[38] Photo: Courtesy Everett Collection / Mondadori Portfolio.

The tomb contains a now-empty burial chamber more than 260 square feet with an arched ceiling nearly 16 feet high, and it must be reached by a 40-foot tunnel (Figure 2.14).

Figure 2.14. The 40-foot entry tunnel (left) into the burial chamber of Cestius' tomb. Photos: Robert Lerner.[39]

Novelty of Eurysaces' Design

Eurysaces did not monopolize size or uniqueness, as Rome's wealthy strove to construct tombs of great notoriety. However, Eurysaces, unlike Caecilia Metella and Cestius, did not stop with simply supersizing his tomb; he strengthened his creation's uniqueness by adopting a design for his tomb that incorporated physical elements of his occupation— baking. Figure 2.15 shows the tomb as it stands in Rome today.

Figure 2.15. The vertical columns and the horizontal cylindrical elements of Eurysaces' tomb that have perplexed scholars since the tomb was rediscovered in 1838. In the late third century AD, the tomb was incorporated into a tower that was part of the city's defensive wall.[40] Photo: Robert Lerner.

The vertical columns were constructed "by stacking three kneading machines (Figure 2.16),"[41] but for the nearly two centuries since the tomb's rediscovery in 1838, historians have debated the horizontal cylindrical elements of the tomb's structure. Arguments for the identification have been made that range from "vents for an oven, grain measures or storage containers, and grinding and cooking machines."[42] As recently as 1993, Olle Brandt, in an article, "Recent Research on the Tomb of Eurysaces," wrote, "All scholars agree that they (the cylinders) must represent some instrument used in a bakery, but no agreement has been found . . . ."[43]

By 2003, however, the tomb design debate seems to have been put to rest by Professor Lauren Hackworth Peterson in her article, "The Baker, His Tomb, His Wife and Her Breadbasket: The Monument of Eurysaces in Rome." In this article, Dr. Peterson argues that the cylinders were not just representations of baking implements; they were *recreated*, large-scale, bread-kneading basins turned on their sides.

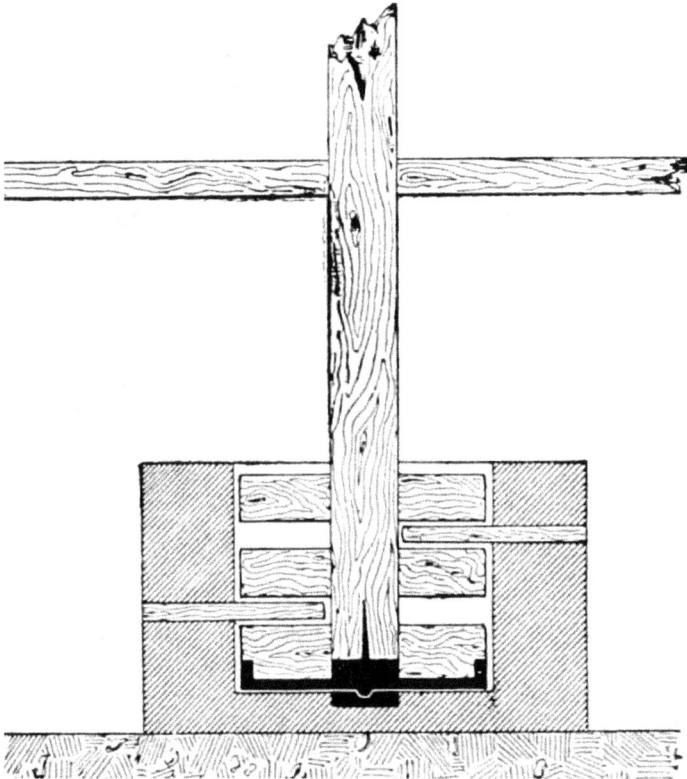

Figure 2.16. A drawing of Roman kneading equipment found in Pompeii. The horizontal cylinders built into Eurysaces' tomb represented the basins in which the kneading paddles turned. Drawing from August Mau, Pompeii: Its Life and Art (New York, 1899), fig. 214.

Dr. Peterson found the horizontal cylinders in the tomb contained square depressions with rust stains that "suggest[s] that in antiquity the depression supported a metal mount for a wooden axis . . . ."[44] The metal mount is the darker element seen at the bottom of the basin depicted in Figure 2.16. Thus, the cylinders are identical to functioning

baking equipment seen in ancient bakeries, except
that they were made of a higher quality of material
(travertine)[45]—Eurysaces wanted realistic baking
imagery, and he projected it with a building material
that further demonstrated his wealth.[46] Such a
kneading machine can be seen in one frieze carved
into the top of Eurysaces' tomb (the far right portion
of the image in Figure 2.17). These friezes will be
discussed in detail in chapter 2.

*Figure 2.17. A frieze on Eurysaces' tomb depicting various
elements of the baking process. The bread-kneading machine
can be seen on the right. It also seems that a horse might have
been used to turn the vertical element of the kneading equipment.
Photo: Robert Lerner.*

Dr. Petersen also says, "The incorporation
of everyday objects for constructive reuse on a
tomb is to my knowledge unique in funerary
architecture, and must have seemed novel to a
viewer, perhaps even humorous."[47] Thus, we see that
with recognizable baking instruments in his tomb's
design and construction, Eurysaces demonstrated
another key CA lesson in gaining an audience's
attention.

Lesson 3: Alter the Familiar for Impact

By studying what is well known to a potential customer and then altering the familiar, such as a cultural icon, famous image, or even familiar baking implements, an advertisement can yield a dramatic impact on the viewer. David Ogilvy, when discussing impactful poster advertisements (which in effect is what Eurysaces' tomb was), colorfully indicated that the images' creative effect should be a "visual scandal."[48]

Paul Messaris extensively discusses this practical point made by Ogilvy in his text *Visual Persuasion: The Role of Images in Advertis*ing. Messaris analyzes the power of using icons and their parody in advertising, such as in Figure 2.18. Messaris points out that by altering a familiar iconic image, such as the Mona Lisa, the advertiser creates ". . . an eye-catching departure from the appearance of a previously familiar object . . . ."[49] The ad immediately strikes a chord and leaves a powerful impression, and the modern consumer's response might be similar to that created by Eurysaces in his efforts to attract an ancient viewer by presenting an oddly shaped tomb constructed from familiar baking instruments.[50]

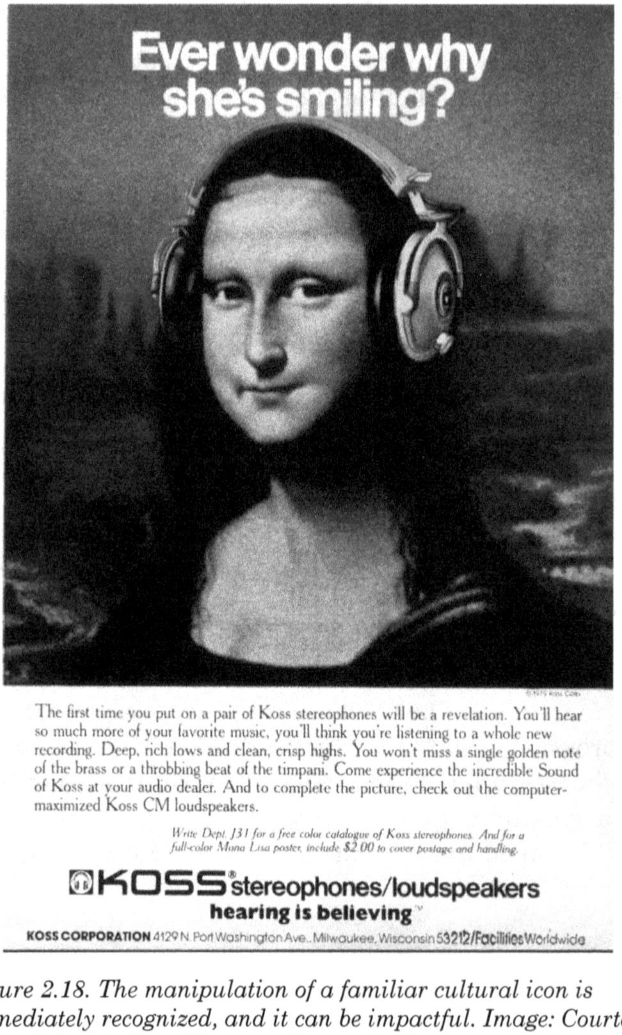

Figure 2.18. The manipulation of a familiar cultural icon is immediately recognized, and it can be impactful. Image: Courtesy Advertising Archive/Courtesy Everett Collection.

Chapter Conclusion

In this chapter, we saw the importance of bread to the ancient Romans and the potential wealth that could be generated from bread-baking business activities, as indicated by the scale of Eurysaces' tomb. From Eurysaces' actions revolving around the planning, design, location, and sizing of his tomb, we developed three lessons focused on Stage 1 of the customer acquisition process—attracting attention (Figure 2.19).

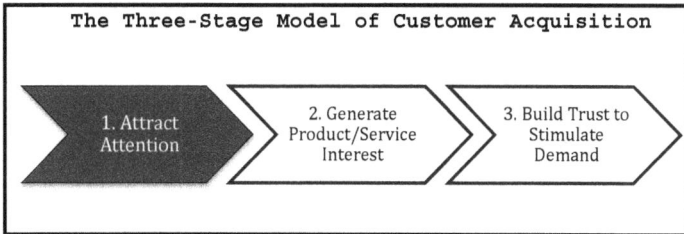

Figure 2.19. The first stage of customer acquisition extensively discussed in this chapter. Eurysaces' tomb construction provided insight into his methods of attracting attention to his business and his success.

The three lessons we formulated dealt with the importance of thorough planning (especially in the early stages), the need to generate some separation from your competition, and the benefits of using familiar or iconic images to generate customer attention and retention. The following summarize these lessons:

Table 2.1. Summary of Chapter 1 Lessons

Lesson	Stage 1: Create Customer Attention
1	Plan Thoroughly
2	Seek Separation from the Pack
3	Alter the Familiar for Impact

CHAPTER 2

Eurysaces (Part 2)

W e will next examine the inscriptions on
Eurysaces' tomb to determine what they
tell about the tomb's owner, his business,
and his customer acquisition efforts. Unfortunately,
only three of the four façades still have remnants
of the ancient inscriptions, and of those, only one
remains in its entirety.

However, based on the elements of the three
inscriptions that remain, length-dependent
variations of the *same* inscription were made on each
side so the message or messages Eurysaces desired
to deliver would be seen and read consistently
regardless of the direction from which the tomb was
viewed. (Figure 2.9 showed how viewers on each
of the two roads next to the tomb had a different
perspective of the edifice.)

The surviving complete inscription is usually translated as follows:[1]

> *This is the monument of*
> *Marcus Vergilius Eurysaces,*
> *baker, contractor, public servant.*

Because of uncertainty of the meaning of the last Latin word (*apparet*) in the surviving inscription (Figure 3.1), there are alternative translations and much scholarly debate replacing "public servant" with either the phrase "it appears" or "it is obvious."

Figure 3.1. Part of the longer inscription on Eurysaces' tomb. Following the name (Marge)i Vergilei Eurysacis (Marcus Vergilius Eurysaces) can be seen the words pistoris (baker), redemptoris (contractor), and apparet (public servant, or it appears, or is obvious). Photo: Robert Lerner.

Eurysaces' communications medium severely limited his ability to alter his inscriptions once executed, and so he must have determined early in the process to repetitively stay "on message" across all the tomb sides. Regardless of the meaning of the long inscription's final words, this replication of similar messages on multiple sides, which viewers could read aloud,[2] offers our fourth customer acquisition lesson from Eurysaces and his tomb.

Lesson 4: Repetition Builds Absorption

The critical element here for the businessperson, especially where modern media and technology offer the ability to change messages as rapidly as funding allows, is to repeat the message for as long as the advertising campaign remains effective. David Ogilvy insisted that if you have a good advertisement, "repeat it until it stops pulling."[3] Ogilvy further reinforced this mantra by noting "... golden rewards await the advertiser who has the brains to create a coherent image, and the stability to stick with it over a long period."[4] Figure 3.2 shows the path to Ogilvy's "golden rewards," along which sellers seek to move consumers with their advertising campaigns.

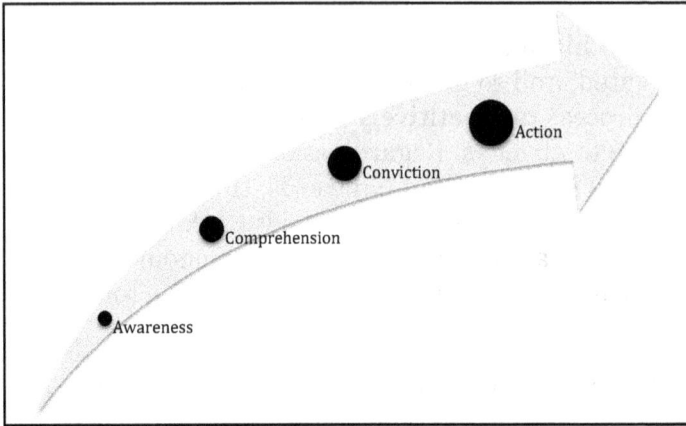

Figure 3.2. Model of how sellers, through ongoing advertising, desire to move consumers forward to a positive purchasing decision (Ogilvy's "golden rewards"). A limitation of this "transport model" is assuming a consumer's inherent passivity in the buying process, but this model's strength is the ability of advertisers to measure, at each stage, the success of advertising campaigns in moving consumers forward to a purchase. [5]

The Campbell's Soup Example

Perhaps one of the most successful practitioners of this consistent approach to advertising is Campbell's® (the Campbell Soup Company) whose soups have been a staple of the American household since 1869, and which has for more than a century sold its soups in the distinctive red-and-white cans (Figure 3.3).

Figure 3.3. A 1920s Campbell's Soup advertisement brightly featuring a red-and-white can similar to that used today. The iconic red-and-white Campbell's Soup cans have been consistently used for more than a century. Image: Courtesy Advertising Archive/Courtesy Everett Collection.

The Implications of Eurysaces' Epitaph

Eurysaces' epitaph provides critical biographical information about the tomb's owner. Although the inscription does not explicitly describe Eurysaces as a former slave,[6] as discussed in the last chapter, his name and occupation suggest a freedman.[7]

Eurysaces listed his occupation as a baker first, then his work as a bread or grain contractor (perhaps to the army or as part of the public dole),[8] and last, his role as a public servant (who perhaps could claim credit for helping feed the Roman people during grain shortages).[9] The order of this list of accomplishments possibly indicates that Eurysaces' baking occupation was the most important of his achievements and his most significant role in society.[10]

Eurysaces Compensates for Limited Literacy

Only a limited few would have read and understood Eurysaces' inscribed epitaph because the literacy rate, although high for ancient Rome's elite, is estimated to have been just 10%–15% of the population.[11] Eurysaces, likely aware that many viewers of his tomb were illiterate, solved this limitation by complementing the written word with images.[12]

Eurysaces' stonemasons carved a series of friezes around the tomb's upper story with occupational images of the baking processes involved in bread making (Figures 3.4 and 3.5). According to Petersen, Eurysaces' tomb was "one of the first not only to represent scenes of bread making but also to depict scenes of work in general on his funerary monument."[13]

Additionally, Petersen reports that paint traces have been found on the frieze, indicating "that the entire frieze was painted to increase legibility for someone standing at the base of the monument."[14] Eurysaces' novel use of occupational images was critical to the delivery of his message about his enterprise's scope and success.

Figure 3.4. Image of the work associated with bread making. From right to left, the frieze depicts officials recording grain receipts, grinding, sieving, and an official inspecting the sieving's quality.[15] Note the image of officials in togas (third from left and far right). The short figure behind the leftmost man in the toga was likely his slave. Photo: Robert Lerner.

Figure 3.5. From right to left, the kneading of the dough with a kneading machine, the making of loaves, and the bread baking.[16] Photo: Robert Lerner.

Ogilvy Comments on Factory Images

The images Eurysaces selected perhaps offered the same message to his ancient customers that modern consumers seek—a testimonial to a manufacturer's abilities to produce the desired product, in Eurysaces' pioneering case, bread. Not surprisingly, David Ogilvy had a tongue-in-cheek opinion on using factories in ads, which he provided with the following limerick:

> *When the client moans and sighs,*
> *make his logo twice the size,*
> *if he should still prove refractory*
> *show a picture of his factory.*
> *Only on the gravest cases*
> *should you show the clients' faces.[17]*

Modern Advertisements Depict Occupational Scenes

Eurysaces' use of colorful and detailed images related to his occupation has a modern flavor. Looking at modern ads, we frequently see proud depictions of state-of-the art production facilities, but this modern trend, although not attributed by anyone directly to Eurysaces, has roots that go at least as far back as the 1800s (Figure 3.6).

Figure 3.6. Shows an image of a Spaulding & Hodge paper manufacturing plant in 1883. Image: Courtesy Mary Evans Picture Library/Everett Collection.

Eurysaces' creative use of inscribed elements and occupational imagery to describe the scope of his industrial abilities brings us to our next lesson in customer recruitment according to Eurysaces.

Lesson 5: Provide the Facts

Eurysaces factually described himself as a baker in text and images. David Ogilvy also demanded that the advertisements his firm produced be factual, for he preached, "The more you tell, the more you sell,"[18] and proclaimed, ". . . the consumer isn't a moron."[19] Ogilvy so trusted the consumer to make an informed decision that he did not shy from giving abundant facts to the consumer when he thought the situation demanded it.

His advertisement in Figure 3.7, considered a classic example of effective advertising copy, consisted of 1,909 words. The discriminating consumer will ultimately abandon a vendor whose message diverges from reality. We cannot know with any certainty whether Eurysaces did his best to convey the truth with his tomb. We know, however, from his tomb's size that he was successful, but we have no data other than what he left us to determine whether that success was based on something less than integrity.

How to create advertising that sells

by David Ogilvy

Figure 3.7. A reproduction of an Ogilvy ad (part of a series on creating powerful advertisements) without using any images and consisting of just 1,909 words of copy.

Eurysaces' Messages for the Viewer

As discussed earlier, an important message for any slave or ex-slave was to display his occupational status in and to society for remembrance— something Eurysaces accomplished. A second message in the case of Eurysaces was to display the scope of his enterprise and his wealth, thereby demonstrating his elite economic status as well.

A third important message is delivered to the viewer through the friezes. Including togate officials in Eurysaces' depiction of the baking processes[20] not only demonstrated a pride in his involvement with the state, but was also likely a powerful *testimonial* to Eurysaces' honesty (and influence) as a baker and public servant. Figure 3.8 shows an enlargement of one of the toga-clad figures shown in Figure 3.4.

Figure 3.8. An enlargement of the toga-clad man and his slave depicted on one of Eurysaces' friezes. Likely, this depicts an inspection by a government official. In an additional frieze involving the weighing of bread, three additional toga-clad officials oversee the weighing process. Photo: Robert Lerner.

This innovative use of togate images provided a powerful message of competency for the viewer, bringing us to the sixth CA lesson from Eurysaces' tomb.

Lesson 6: Leverage Testimonials

Eurysaces' tomb, decorated with the men in togas, perhaps offers history's first example, in what has become a long line, of celebrity testimonials or famous spokespersons in advertisements. David Ogilvy, in discussing his experience with television commercials, noted, "The use of unusual characters increases the power of commercials to change brand preference by a remarkably high percentage."[21]

An Example of an Iconic Testimonial

A modern example of such a testimonial can be seen in Figure 3.9, where an endorsement for the product in the ad is made by a cultural icon—Santa Claus. This type of advertisement, much like Eurysaces' testimonial, has stood the test of time, for Santa has been used successfully in modern print and television advertisements to hawk everything from soda to automobiles for decades.

Figure 3.9. Santa enjoying (and endorsing) a bottle of Coke, a trend that has continued over many decades. Image: Courtesy Advertising Archive/Courtesy Everett Collection.

A Second Example of an Iconic Testimonial

The advertisement in Figure 3.10 uses the same approach as in the above ad, and as surprising as the ad now seems to us, it might have been successful in the 1930s. However, unlike Eurysaces' testimonial, this Santa ad has not stood the test of time, for it now seems jarring and in poor taste.

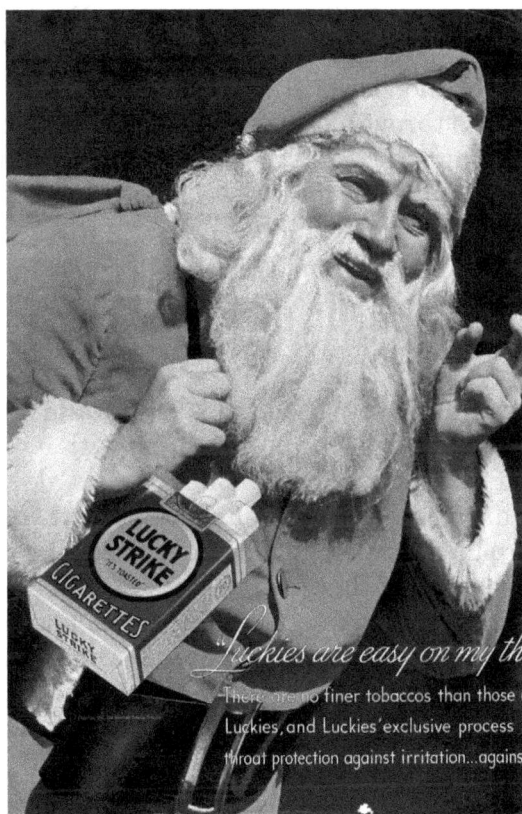

Figure 3.10. The jarring image of Santa enjoying a Lucky Strike. In the 1930s, this advertisement would have generated a much more favorable response from the consumer. Image: Courtesy Advertising Archive/Courtesy Everett Collection.

An Ancient Viewer of Eurysaces' Tomb

Now, imagine a Roman citizen approaching Eurysaces' tomb. From a distance, the ancient viewer was first struck by the monument's size and peculiar structure composed of baking implements. After closer examination, the brightly colored frieze images were seen and perhaps even complemented by the sound of other viewers reading aloud Eurysaces' epitaph. Taken all together, Eurysaces more than successfully created Ogilvy's "visual scandal" for the viewer. Eurysaces' reinforcement of his message through multiple media—text to be read aloud, vibrant frieze images, and the tomb's unique structure assaulting the eyes—brings us to our next CA lesson.

Lesson 7: Assault the Consumer's Senses

Eurysaces effectively used the media available—a stone tomb—to engage viewers' eyes (with its shape and images) and ears (with epitaphs read aloud) to deliver his message to his audience. If fruit trees or other aromatic growth had been planted near the tomb, the scent of the trees or plants might also have further reinforced the tomb's impact on the passersby's senses.[22] Aromatic fauna would perhaps be less an "assault" on the senses than a seduction.

Aromatic Advertising

Modern advertisers have diligently sought better means to assault and appeal to consumers' senses (both figuratively and literally). One late twentieth-century entry was the advent of scratch-and-sniff technology to impart on a consumer the fragrance of the product available for purchase. A recent study showed a nearly 20% improvement in an advertisement's "stopping power" with the addition of a scent, although it never achieved great acceptance.[23] A French winery creatively used smell to help market their wine (Figure 2.11). A master sommelier has even authored a scratch-and-sniff book for students of winetasting (*The Essential Scratch and Sniff Guide* to Becoming *a Wine Expert: Take a Whiff of That* by Richard Betts).

Figure 3.11. A scratch-and-sniff label on a bottle of French wine produced by Domaine Bourillion Dorleans. "Terroir Vouvray is a French term that encompasses natural factors contributing to the distinctiveness of wine."[24] Photo: Courtesy of Jameson Fink, 2011.

The combined impact of the multiple elements of Eurysaces' message (likely with everything baking-related, except the scent of fresh bread) powerfully reminds us that a consumer's attention can be captured with stimuli targeted at several senses.

The Final Message of Eurysaces' Tomb

Eurysaces was not finished with his efforts to deliver a consistent message to his audience and to posterity. On the third story of the tomb's no longer extant side, a statue of Eurysaces and his wife, Atista, was thought to stand, along with an epitaph for his wife (Figure 3.12).

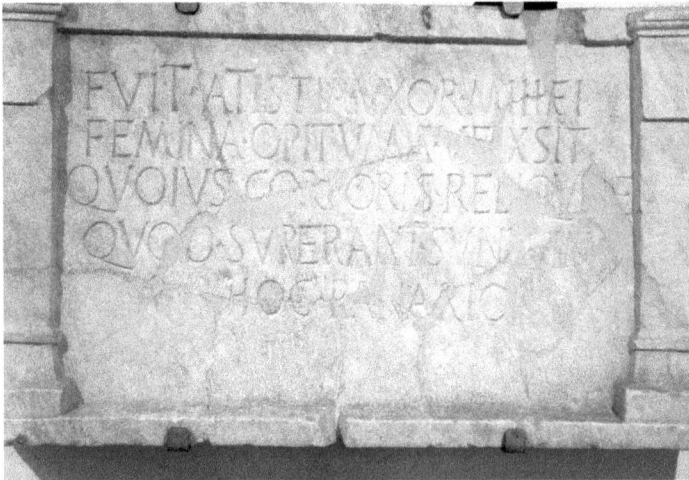

Figure 3.12. Eurysaces' reconstructed epitaph for his wife, Atista, housed in the National Roman Museum (Baths of Diocletian/ The Epigraphic Museum). Photo: Robert Lerner.

Eurysaces' epitaph for his wife, when translated, reads:

> *Atista was my wife. She lived as awonderful woman, the remains of whose body which survive are in this breadbasket.*[25]

Eurysaces' epitaph for his wife not only shows his devotion to his wife, but also unequivocally demonstrates the passion, if not obsession, Eurysaces had for his baking business (his wife likely predeceased him and, hence, could not complain of any of the tomb's design features or her epitaph).[26]

I earlier referenced a quote from Professor Petersen indicating passersby might have seen baking instruments humorously included in the tomb's construction. If so, combined with the potential for additional lighthearted image-making for the containment of Atista's ashes, we see Eurysaces' creative humor to further engage the viewer. Humor offers us our eighth CA lesson from Eurysaces.

Lesson 8: Engage a Viewer with Humor

Again, we turn to David Ogilvy for insights on humor in customer recruitment. Ogilvy reported that research shows advertising that contains humor could influence consumer buying.[27] However, Ogilvy also warned that it is difficult to be funny and that "people don't buy from clowns."[28]

We cannot know whether Eurysaces intended to be humorous with his tomb's elements, or he was deadly serious about his work, but we view his efforts humorously now. Humor is often in the eye of the beholder, but to demonstrate humor's potential power to quickly engage the viewer in an advertisement, I offer the advertisement in Figure 3.13.

Alka-Seltzer

On The Rocks

You haven't tried it yet?
Oh boy.
Alka-Seltzer On The Rocks works just like Alka-Seltzer Off The Rocks...only it's good enough to drink. Maybe even delicious? And it relieves an upset stomach and summer

headache faster...
better than anything you can buy without a prescription. Try it at a picnic. Try it at the beach. Plop two Alka-Seltzers in water. Let it bubble a few seconds. Add ice. A slice of lime. Cheers.

Figure 3.13. Humor's immediate impact (and the alteration of the familiar) on the viewer in an Alka-Seltzer print ad. Image: Advertising Archive/Courtesy of Everett Collection.

This classic Alka-Seltzer ad engages the viewer with its gentle humor by depicting the cure for overdoing one's alcohol consumption in a fashion as enticing as an alcoholic beverage itself.

Eurysaces' Tomb Construction before His Death

We have made much of Eurysaces' marketing abilities, but we might ask how effective a tomb would be if it were only constructed after its builder's death. Most slaves and ex-slaves, because of their extreme poverty as seen earlier in the text, were fortunate to have any monument to their life constructed after their death. However, a uniquely determined and financially well-to-do ex-slave such as Eurysaces might begin construction of a funerary monument before his demise; for the wealthy, "it was common for people to oversee the construction of their own tombs before death."[29]

The financial ability to begin construction before one's death helped ensure the tomb was properly constructed,[30] reflected the deceased's final wishes, and mitigated any after-death legal complications that might postpone the tomb's construction. Eurysaces, although no aristocrat, was wealthy enough to begin construction before his death, and given Atista's epitaph indicating that she predeceased Eurysaces and the obsessive detailing of the tomb's baking references, Eurysaces most likely began his tomb's construction well before his death.

There are two additional reasons to assume the structure was constructed while Eurysaces lived:

1. Eurysaces began his epitaph with the unique phrasing "This is the monument of"—possibly indicating that the tomb was what it claimed—a monument to Eurysaces designed to commemorate his life and business more than his death.[31]

2. Eurysaces' desire to display his success seems unbounded, and the tomb (as well as its construction) offered an acceptable means to generate attention while he was alive.

Thus, Eurysaces likely did not pass up the opportunity to use his funerary monument as a testimony to himself and his business while he was alive.

The Emperor Augustus' Tomb Construction

Perhaps one of the longest periods between construction and internment was for the Emperor Augustus himself, whose completed mausoleum accepted the remains of a nephew of his in 23 BC, but did not welcome the Emperor himself until AD 14, nearly four decades later![32] Figure 3.14 shows a model of Augustus' circular tomb as it is thought to have appeared in Rome at the time of its construction (nearly 300 feet in diameter, possibly more than 10 stories tall, and dotted with trees).

Figure 3.14. A model of Emperor Augustus' tomb as it is thought to have appeared at the time of its construction in 23 BC. Despite its diminutive appearance in the photograph, the mausoleum when constructed spanned more than a football field in diameter. The tomb was crowned with a statue of Augustus that was likely melted in the Middle Ages.[33] The model is in Rome's Ara Pacis Museum. Photo: Robert Lerner.

Unfortunately, the passage of time has not been as kind to the Emperor Augustus' tomb as it has that of Eurysaces. The current state of that tomb, which has served over the intervening two millennia since its construction as a marble workshop, "a fortress for the Colonna family, a hanging garden, a bullring, amphitheater, and concert hall,"[34] can be seen in Figure 3.15.

Figure 3.15. The Emperor Augustus' tomb in its state of disrepair as of 2013. Photo: Robert Lerner.

Eurysaces' Tomb and Rome's Elite

Rome's elite likely perceived the messages communicated by the ex-slave Eurysaces' tomb, and the messages repelled them. An ancient literary example demonstrating many aspects of elite disdain for the accomplishments and actions of upstart freedmen can be found in *The Satyricon,* a first-century AD novel by Gaius Petronius Arbiter. This Petronius might have been part of the Emperor Nero's inner circle (Nero ruled Rome from AD 54–68).

Petronius' writing shows that he shared the upper classes' great distaste for *nouveau riche* ex-slaves as well as "vulgar" tradesmen. Petronius created a literary character Trimalchio, and Trimalchio, like Eurysaces, was a fabulously wealthy former slave who wanted to build a funerary monument of monolithic proportions before his death. Petronius contemptuously depicted Trimalchio as an ignorant and buffoonish businessperson who thought his tomb should rival an emperor's tomb. (See Appendix A.) Then, to ensure that his funerary lampoon was complete, Petronius included an occupational epitaph that said of Trimalchio:

> *He died a millionaire,*
> *Though he started life with nothing.*[35]

Thus, all are reminded for perpetuity that the wealthy freedman began as a slave with nothing and as nothing in Roman society.

However exaggerated and sarcastic the fictional Trimalchio's depiction is, we can assume more than a bit of reality drawn from the wealthy ex-slaves of Imperial Rome of the early/middle first century AD and, hence, generations of scholars' efforts to extend a link from the fictional Trimalchio further back to Eurysaces (a wealthy ex-slave in the late first century BC). Regardless of how tenuous the connections between Trimalchio and Eurysaces, the elite's outrage at upstart ex-slaves was real. Thus, the outrage likely generated by Eurysaces' visible tomb establishes this chapter's next CA lesson.

Lesson 9: Outrage Garners Attention

From a marketing perspective, if Eurysaces' tomb was in any way responsible for a powerful imperial advisor to fulminate against the predilections of wealthy ex-slaves, then Eurysaces' campaign for attention was extraordinarily effective and successful. Today, advertisements that push the boundaries of acceptability seem more the norm than the exception, and nothing exemplifies that fact more than jeans manufacturers' advertising efforts.

Over a decade before Calvin Klein's iconic 1980 TV campaign with the 15-year-old Brooke Shields ("You want to know what comes between me and my Calvins? Nothing!") generated its desired outrage, Wrangler, the venerable manufacturer of jeans for cowboys used nudity to expand its market (Figure 3.16).

Because outrage can also produce a backlash, we must again look to David Ogilvy for guidance. We find that he reminded advertisers that they should "never write an advertisement you wouldn't want your own family to read."[36] Thus, we have reasonable boundaries for using outrage—sufficient to garner attention and insufficient to offend.

Waiting for Wrangler

The naked truth. Cover it with Wranglers. Made for the tough or soft life in denim or corduroy. Make the scene in a new pair of jeans in parallels or flares with jackets to match. In a choice of 13 mind-blowing shades—like red, lemon, petrol blue, loden, wheat, white, black, rosé, navy and antelope. Available throughout the country. For illustrated brochure, send postcard to: Wrangler Jeans, Dept. N1, Blue Bell, Colwick Industrial Estate, Nottingham, NG4 2DP.

Jeans and jackets from

Wrangler

Denim and corduroy

Figure 3.16. An edgy Wrangler jeans ad from the 1960s. Image: Courtesy Advertising Archive / Everett Collection).

Consistency of Message

Regardless of the underlying drivers (humor or seriousness) for Eurysaces' design of his tomb, the baking elements incorporated in the tomb, with the breadbasket, the epitaph, the frieze, and portraiture, powerfully demonstrate the total integration of the tomb's communicative power to describe the life, wealth, occupation, and scope of Eurysaces' business interests. This unified approach yields our final Stage 1 customer acquisition lesson from Eurysaces and his tomb.

Lesson 10: Ensure Message Consistency

The lesson here does not mean that you must use all available media (and we have a much more expansive set of alternatives than those available to Eurysaces), rather your message must remain unified across whichever media are used.

David Ogilvy provides insight into the rationale for the need to ensure one's message is consistent across multiple communications vehicles when he discusses his efforts to reach the typical homemaker of the mid-twentieth century. Ogilvy advises, "Your advertisement should establish in the reader's mind an image which she will never forget."[37]

If messages are not mutually reinforcing, or they are incoherent, the probability of delivering an unforgettable image is low. Given the difficulty of displaying multimedia ads on the printed page, I instead offer here another advertisement (Figure 3.17) done by Ogilvy for McGraw-Hill magazines, which further demonstrates the need for consistency of message during the complex process of customer acquisition.

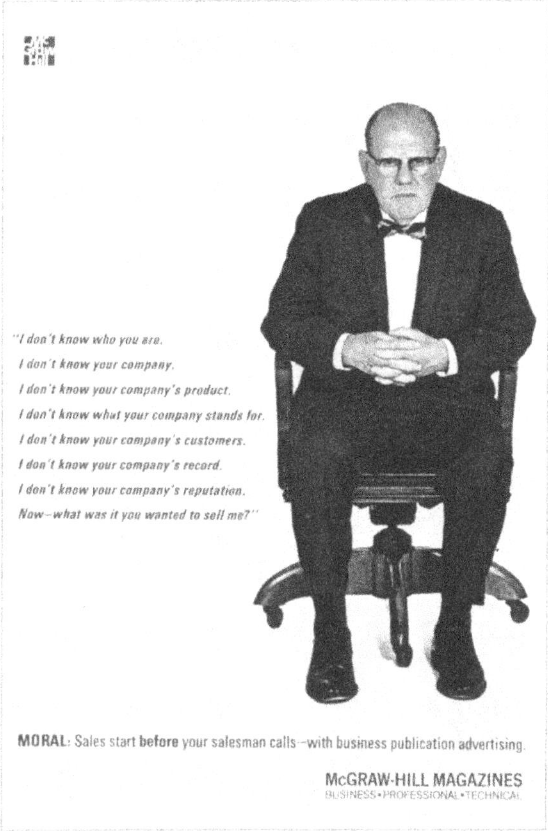

Figure 3.17. An Ogilvy ad for McGraw-Hill Publications, stating the importance of integrated communication to a potential customer. Image: Advertising Archive/Courtesy Everett Collection.

Chapter Summary

We have now completed our study of Eurysaces the baker, as documented by his elaborate funerary monument. The scale of Eurysaces' business interests is well documented by the visual messages he used to attract his audience's attention.

Eurysaces' innovative efforts to reach that audience, even the illiterate, with the friezes of his baking business, which Petersen describes as "triumphal,"[38] was likely effective because that medium was later used, perhaps to its greatest extent in history, by the Roman Emperor Trajan on his column (Figure 3.18).

Figure 3.18. An early photo (1896) of Trajan's column.[39] The entire 98-foot column is decorated with a continuous frieze depicting Trajan's battles with the Dacians.

Trajan, who ruled Rome from AD 98 to AD 117, completed his triumphal column of visual messages in AD 113. The 98-foot-high column (on a 25-foot-high pedestal) displays a 625-foot continuous frieze that encircles the column twenty-three times.[40] The thousands of figures in the frieze visually narrate Trajan's two brutal wars with the Dacians (the capital of Dacia was in what is now Romania). The column still stands in Rome. Figure 3.19 shows the power of the column's detailed images.

Figure 3.19. Details of Trajan's visual messages about his legions and the war in Dacia contained in his column's frieze. This photo is of a plaster cast of the original column housed in London's Victoria and Albert Museum. Photo: Robert Lerner.

Eurysaces accomplished with his tomb, as Trajan did with his column, what so many advertisers have striven for and continue to strive for—a powerful and convincing message with a long shelf life that successfully attracts the viewer's attention (Figure 3.20).

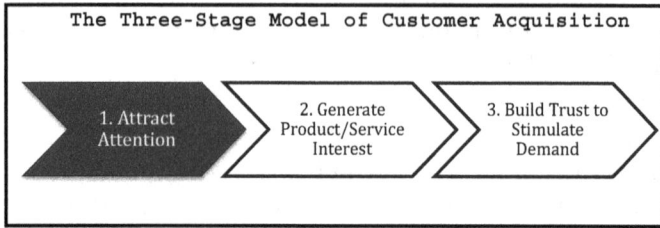

The Three-Stage Model of Customer Acquisition

1. Attract Attention

2. Generate Product/Service Interest

3. Build Trust to Stimulate Demand

Figure 3.20. Highlights the first stage of customer acquisition discussed in this chapter.

By examining the epitaphs and friezes on Eurysaces' tomb, we also formulated seven Stage 1 customer acquisition lessons, enumerated in Table 3.1.

Table 3.1. Summary of Chapter 2 Lessons

Lesson	Stage 1: Create Customer Attention
4	Repetition Builds Absorption
5	Provide the Facts
6	Leverage Testimonials
7	Assault the Consumer's Senses
8	Engage a Viewer with Humor
9	Outrage Can Be Effective
10	Ensure Message Consistency

CHAPTER 3

Eumachia

Today, perhaps the best-known symbol of daily life in ancient Rome is the toga (which typically required 12 feet by 18 feet of woolen cloth).[1] The toga-draped official was an important element depicted on Eurysaces' tomb (Figures 3.4 and 3.8) and on the surviving friezes of the Emperor Augustus' family (Figure 4.1).[2] Rome's male citizens wore togas at public events, and Vergil, in the *Aeneid*, his epic poem about Rome's founding, wrote that the gods "cherish as world rulers those men in their togas."[3]

Figure 4.1. Agrippa (left), the Emperor Augustus' son-in-law, in his toga during a religious procession, displayed on the Ara Pacis (Altar of Augustan Peace). Photo: Courtesy of Shutterstock.

In Emperor Augustus' Rome, women, except prostitutes, could not wear a toga, but they could, and likely did, contribute to the production of togas (and other woolen garments), not production in the modern mechanistic sense, but in the ancient manual weaving process.

Roman wives and daughters were idealized as spending their leisure time making homespun garments. An ancient writer even noted that the Emperor Augustus "wore common clothes for the house, made by his sister, wife, daughter or grand-daughters."[4]

However, by the middle of the first century AD, under the Emperor Nero, one ancient writer complained, "Ladies would not be bothered with weaving and bought expensive clothes instead."[5] However, this proclivity did not stop wealthy households from owning slaves who wove.[6]

Multiple Steps in Wool Garment Production

Because togas were made of wool, their creation began with the raising and shearing of sheep whose fleece ultimately rode on the shoulders of the "world rulers." In ancient Rome, much like today, the production of fleece into a wool garment consisted of several steps that began with sheepherding and ended with woolen yarn, woven fabric, or a completed garment available for sale to the consumer. The typical steps are depicted in Figure 4.2.

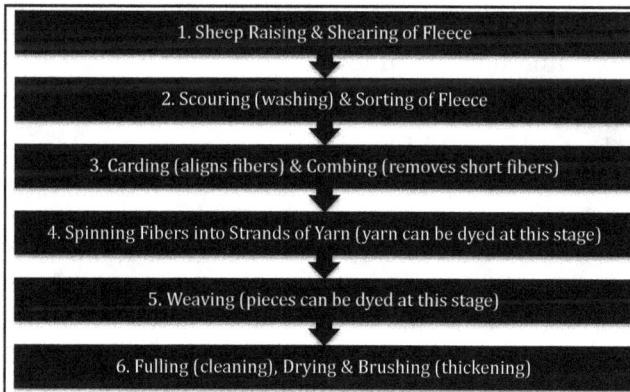

1. Sheep Raising & Shearing of Fleece
2. Scouring (washing) & Sorting of Fleece
3. Carding (aligns fibers) & Combing (removes short fibers)
4. Spinning Fibers into Strands of Yarn (yarn can be dyed at this stage)
5. Weaving (pieces can be dyed at this stage)
6. Fulling (cleaning), Drying & Brushing (thickening)

Figure 4.2. Steps involved in the production of woolen fabric (for example, for a toga).

In ancient Rome, the work associated with steps 1 to 4 seems to not have had much formal organization (for example, guild), and no tombstones recall the labor of a carder or spinner.[7] However, the fulling and dying trades were distinct and well organized.[8] Archeological evidence in Pompeii shows eleven fulleries and six textile-dyeing facilities.[9] Garment production was very likely a significant part of the Pompeian economy and many other Roman cities and towns, based on the number of textile-related production facilities and many identified locations.[10]

Eumachia and Her Position in Pompeian Society

Fortunately, as with Eurysaces, we can learn much about our next entrepreneur and her business life from the inscriptions and edifices she left us. We know that Eumachia was the daughter of Lucius Eumachius, who owned a brickyard[11] and whose wealthy family can be "traced back to early Greek settlers who grew rich on the land; wine jars bearing their name have been found in southern France."[12]

Eumachia's husband, Numistrius Frontones, who likely predeceased her, was from one of the oldest families in Pompeii with large interests in sheep and the wool trade.[13] Eumachia had at least one son, Marcus Numistrius Fronto, and we know that Eumachia, like her mother, was a priestess of a cult of the goddess Venus.

Eumachia's Building

One of Pompeii's largest buildings stood at one edge of the city's Forum (marketplace).[14] Excavated between 1814 and 1822, "it is called the Building of Eumachia after the priestess of the municipal cult who built the edifice and dedicated it in her name and that of her son."[15] It turns out that determining who built the structure has been somewhat simpler than determining its function, for scholars have debated the use of Eumachia's magnificent benefaction for the last two centuries. The site plan for the huge building (160 feet x 80 feet) is shown in Figure 4.3.[16]

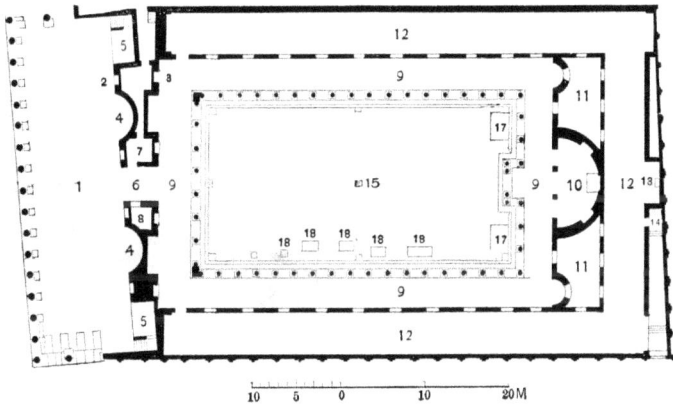

Figure 4.3. The site plan for the Building of Eumachia.[17] A statue of Eumachia was found in a rear niche (13). The building's portico (1), containing a partial surviving inscription, faced the city's Forum, and a second inscription, surviving in its entirety, was found above the entrance shown in the plan's lower right corner.[18] The large niche (10) held a statue of the goddess Concordia Augusta.[19]

The edifice is thought to have resembled the architectural rendering in Figure 4.4, and despite its current disrepair, the building's original grandeur can still be appreciated from the structure's colonnades that remain in the Forum of Pompeii as shown in Figure 4.5. The date of the building's dedication has been much debated, but Walter O. Moeller, in his book *The Wool Trade of Ancient Pompeii,* persuasively argues for construction under way in 2 BC and "ready for dedication in AD 3/4,"[20] during the Emperor Augustus' reign.

Figure 4.4. An architectural rendering of the Building of Eumachia as it might have looked in the first century AD.[21]

Figure 4.5. The current state of the Building of Eumachia.[22] *The structure's colonnades (depicted in location (1) of Figure 4.3) and portions of the dedicatory inscription can still be seen. Photo: Courtesy of Shutterstock.*

The building's inscription was engraved on two sides of the structure, providing a consistency of message from Eumachia that was like Eurysaces' communication efforts on his tomb. Parts of the inscription can be seen in Figure 4.5 and in its entirety read:

Eumachia,
daughter of Lucius Eumachius,
a city priestess,
in her own name and that of her son,
Marcus Numistrius Fronto,
built at her own expense
the portico, the corridor, and the colonnade,
dedicating them to Concordia Augusta and Pietas.[23]

(Author's Note: Concordia Augusta was an aspect of the goddess Concordia referring to family harmony, and Pietas, the ideal relationship among parents and children, men and gods, and men and the state.[24])

Given the size (multistoried and one of the city's largest) and location of the structure (at a corner of the Forum) that Eumachia, a woman, chose to build for Pompeii's residents, likely with bricks from her brickyard, we can formulate our first CA lesson from Eumachia's actions.

Lesson 11: Be Bold

We have seen that Eumachia's building rivaled the size and magnificence of any structures in the city, and by constructing that monument in such a prime location, she ensured its visibility and use by all levels of Pompeian society (as well as visitors of any rank).

Eumachia was not a woman of small vision. Donald Trump, unsurprisingly, has an opinion on the importance of being bold. Trump, in his book *Think Big*, declares that to make an impact and to be successful, you must, like Trump, "Define yourself in a big way."[25] And big is not to be on the surface only—Trump advises that "bigness" must permeate every thought and action, and when you do so, "your confidence will soar."[26]

For an excellent modern example of an advertisement demonstrating the confidence to be bold, I again must refer the reader to the Apple "1984" advertisement in Figure 2.11. That ad not only offered separation from the pack; it was also "revolutionary and astonishing."[27] Steve Jobs overran the resistance of his board of directors and went with the commercial that openly attacked IBM, the market leader in PCs at the time.

After running during the Super Bowl, the advertisement was shown on "all three networks and fifty local stations aired news stories about the ad . . . ."[28] Like Eumachia's building, the bold 1984 Apple ad still generates attention and discussion years after it was first unveiled. Apple reused the ad for the iPod in 2004.

Eumachia's Statue and Its Implications

One key helping to determine the function of Eumachia's building was found in the structure during its excavation. Archeologists discovered an exquisitely preserved statue of Eumachia at location 13 in Figure 4.3. This identification could be positively made because the pedestal on which the statue stood survived, and the translation of the inscription reads as follows:

Dedicated to Eumachia, daughter of Lucius Eumachius, a city priestess, by the fullers.[29]

Figure 4.6. The statue of Eumachia found in her building.[30]
Eumachia is shown wearing a linen stola (like a dress or a long
tunic) with a woven palla over her head and wrapped around her
body. The palla was commonly made of wool and was worn by
women similarly to how men wore a toga.

Thus, we have archeological proof that the statue depicts Eumachia, that she was Lucius Eumachius' daughter, and that she was a city priestess. We also learn from the inscription that Pompeii's fullers honored Eumachia with the statue erected in the building she commissioned. This inscription directly links Eumachia to Pompeii's fullers and establishes the foundation on which scholars have attempted to interpret her building's functionality.

Ancient Fullers

The ancient fuller's work was twofold: 1) to make cloth fresh from the loom ready for use and 2) to cleanse garments that had been worn.[31] The processes associated with the fulling of new cloth are shown in Table 4.1.[32]

Table 4.1. Processes Associated with Fulling New Cloth

Step	Process	Description
1	Washing	Removes oils and dirt
2	Beating/Stretching	Evens the surface of the cloth
3	Washing & Drying	Cleans and shrinks cloth
4	Combing/Brushing	Prepares cloth for shearing
5	Shearing	Reduces cloth surface (nap) to proper length
6	Bleaching	Whitens
7	Pressing	Smoothes the cloth

A reproduction of an ancient Pompeian painting of fullers washing clothes is shown in Figure 4.7. At first glance, it seems that wealthy Eumachia and the fullers were oddly matched collaborators. However, the fullers were a well-organized and critical component of Pompeii's garment industry, possibly controlling the "flow of wool to assure a profitable outcome."[33] Therefore, it is reasonable for Eumachia, the wool magnate, to cultivate a close relationship with the fullers to help protect or grow her market or markets.

Figure 4.7. Four workers are cleaning textiles in vats placed in small niches. The worker standing higher than the others is shown balancing himself by holding on to the niche's low walls.[34] The cleaning solution was often a mixture of water and aged urine.[35] The urine was collected around the city and used because of its ammonia content.

On the other side of the equation, the fullers were much maligned because of the work they did and the chemicals (stale urine) they used. Even the Emperor Vespasian, who ruled Rome from AD 69 to AD 79, joked at their expense to teach his son

Titus a lesson. Vespasian's son complained when his father taxed the contents of Rome's urinals that the fullers used. Vespasian's response was "to hand him a coin that had been part of the first day's proceeds: 'Does it smell bad?' he asked."[36]

Not surprisingly, Pompeii's fullers would have welcomed the support of a powerful patron and erected a statue in that patron's honor—even if that patron was a woman. This close alignment of producer (Eumachia and her wool) and channel partner (the fullers and their services in the woolen textile trade) establishes our second customer acquisition lesson from Eumachia.

Lesson 12: Support Your Channel Partners

Primarily because of the fuller's statue dedicated to Eumachia, current scholarly opinion of the building's function (there is no definitive consensus) is as follows:[37]

1. The building served as an exchange and auction house for Pompeii's wool merchants.

2. The upper stories served as temporary storerooms for textiles (for example, wool).

3. The building served as a guildhall for the city's fullers.

4. The building served as a marketplace for the city's export of wool to other cities.

5. The building was a place for business people to transact business.

6. The building was a retail center for wool and possibly other textiles. (This opinion has been discredited, as has the opinion that the building was a fullery).

Regardless of the specific use and users of the facility, one element is clear—Pompeian fullers were important to Pompeii's wool industry. And if Eumachia kept weavers on her estate, her products would not just have been fleece or yarn, they could also have included woven woolen cloth. With fleece and possibly woolen cloth as major cash crops of Eumachia, not surprisingly, she wisely sought to ensure that the channel partners most critical to her revenue and profits were well cared for (a channel strategy that modern business managers would do well to emulate).[38]

Eumachia's Constraints

Eumachia had challenges that businessmen did not—she was a female in a male-dominated society with clear cultural limitations on what was proper for women. The Emperor Augustus passed a law in 18 BC to encourage (with inducements and penalties) widows between the ages of twenty and fifty to remarry within twelve months of their husband's demise. In AD 9, the window for delay was graciously extended to two years.[39] Supposedly, this, and a requirement that unattached women (without three children) have a male guardian, helped protect a widow's assets.[40]

Managing the home, spinning, and weaving were socially acceptable and honorable; running a business or businesses and donating buildings or portions of buildings was much less so.[41] However, if Eumachia foresaw to expand her number of domestics that wove to industrial-sized proportions, she, ironically, would have engaged in the one business that men would have been hard pressed to criticize—the spinning and weaving of cloth—the centuries-old admired role of a Roman woman.[42] We cannot know whether Eumachia chose this path, but given her familial history with the woolen industry and the size of the building she commissioned, Eumachia likely had her hands in large-scale weaving as well. This approach to determining constraints and finding creative means to move beyond them forms our next customer acquisition lesson.

Lesson 13: Think Outside the Box

Eumachia followed the rules but did so creatively and still managed to have a public and accepted role in society. Perhaps the most relevant modern example of thinking outside the box comes from our generation's greatest product marketer—Steve Jobs. Jobs was so determined to move beyond the ordinary constraints that bind most of us that he even resorted to exhorting his customers to "Think Different" (Figure 4.8).[43]

Figure 4.8. The ad tagline and Apple trademark used by Steve Jobs in their 1997 Think Different advertising campaign.[44]

In a series of ads, Job also used black-and-white photos of cultural icons such as Einstein, Picasso, Edison, Maria Callas, and Amelia Earhart with the Apple logo and the words Think Different.[45] A version of the Think Different television ad featured a reading of the following text by Richard Dreyfuss:[46]

> *Here's to the crazy ones.*
> *The misfits.*
> *The rebels.*
> *The troublemakers.*
> *The round pegs in the square holes.*
> *The ones who see things differently.*
> *They're not fond of rules.*
> *And they have no respect for the status quo.*
> *You can quote them, disagree with them,*
> *glorify or vilify them.*
> *About the only thing you can't do is ignore*
> *them.*
> *Because they change things.*
> *They push the human race forward.*
> *And while some may see them as the crazy*
> *ones, we see genius.*
> *Because the people who are crazy enough to*
> *think they can change the world, are the ones*
> *who do.*

Eumachia seems to have been one of those unique individuals who resisted her societal constraints and thought not just outside the box— she thought different.

Eumachia's Difference

How differently Eumachia thought can be discerned in her building inscription we reviewed. Let's look again at the final portion of her inscription:

. . . built at her own expense the portico, the corridor, and the colonnade, dedicating them to Concordia Augusta and Pietas.

We see that Eumachia did not say she built the entire building at her expense and dedicated it, rather only specific portions of the building, which has led scholars to debate not only the use of the building, but also whether the building was public or private.[47] The building's use might be uncertain, but Eumachia's inscription is not, for the inscription specifically informs the reader only that the portico, corridor, and the colonnade, areas 1, 9, and 12 in Figure 3.3[48] were constructed "at her own expense."

Given the specificity of the inscription's wording, Eumachia likely funded the reconstruction or enhancement of an existing commercial building.[49] The customer acquisition lesson that emerges from this discussion is based on two facts, regardless of the building's use: 1) the funding for its reconstruction came from Eumachia, and 2) the construction expenses were likely enormous, demonstrating that, even in antiquity, generating customer awareness did not come cheap.

Lesson 14: Attracting Customer Attention Is Costly

Eumachia spent huge sums on her building's public (and private) portions. The result was a landmark in Pompeii's Forum. From a modern perspective, what does "not come cheap" mean? For 2012, Nielsen reported that from 2011 to 2012, "globally, ad spending increased 3.2% year-over-year to $557 billion."[50]

If you want to compete in the global marketplace, you should be acutely sensitive to how much you spend on generating customer attention and how that expenditure stacks against competitors and their spending in your marketplace. Customer acquisition is expensive, and if you want to be bold and buy separation from the pack, as Eumachia did nearly 2,000 years ago, it will not come inexpensively or without hard work.

"Live Richly"—The Billion-Dollar Ad Campaign

The bank Citicorp, whose successful "Live Richly" campaign ran from 2001 to 2006, demonstrates how much money can be spent on an advertising campaign. The intent of the advertising campaign, which was perhaps the most expensive in history, was to convince homeowners to tap into the value stored in their homes and to take out home equity loans.

The *New York Times* reported that "[t]he advertising campaign, which cost some $1 billion from 2001 to 2006, urged people to lighten up about money and helped persuade hundreds of thousands of Citi customers to take out home equity loans— that is, to borrow against their homes. As one of the ads proclaimed: 'There's got to be at least $25,000 hidden in your house. We can help you find it.'"[51] Timing was extraordinary—the program wound down as the great recession of 2007/8 began and just before the housing bubble burst, throwing millions of American homeowners into foreclosure.

Eumachia's Accomplishments

Eumachia accomplished much in the male-dominated Roman business world in particular and Roman society in general, running large family enterprises, commissioning and overseeing a huge construction project in the city's central marketplace, and publically aligning herself with the most powerful textile business fraternity in Pompeii. Eumachia also operated as the head of her family and obtained and maintained her position as a priestess in a religious cult.

These accomplishments set a high bar for any modern businessperson looking to acquire a marketplace's attention. For if one, as Donald Trump earlier noted, wishes to be "big," there is no better means of meeting that goal than by serving as a visible leader in your industry or marketplace. The need to strive for leadership establishes our final lesson from Eumachia.

Lesson 15: Be a Leader in Your Marketplace

Eumachia was literally placed on a pedestal by the fullers, and she stood above most citizens, male and female, in ancient Pompeii. Customers in any age innately wish to deal with industry leaders, but as Eumachia demonstrated, leadership requires creativity and immense hard work.

Steve Jobs, perhaps better than anyone, knew what was involved in being an industry leader and a master at generating customer attention, not just for the short term, but also over decades. He shared some of his insights when he delivered the commencement address to the Stanford University 2005 graduating class. Jobs said, "Don't be trapped by dogma—which is living with the results of other people's thinking. Don't let the noise of other's opinions drown out your own inner voice. And most important, have the courage to follow your heart and intuition."[52]

Chapter Summary

In this chapter, we have seen that Pompeii's woolen textile industry was significant and that Eumachia likely played a major role in the marketplace from wool production to patron of the fullers. From her activities, we formulated five Stage 1 CA lessons besides the ten already established in our study of Eurysaces.

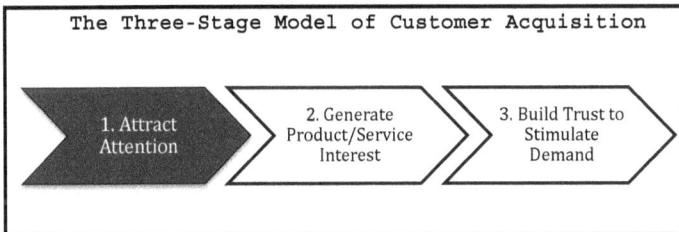

The Three-Stage Model of Customer Acquisition

1. Attract Attention
2. Generate Product/Service Interest
3. Build Trust to Stimulate Demand

Figure 4.9. The first stage of customer acquisition discussed in this chapter. Eumachia's building construction efforts provide insight into her methods of attracting attention, supporting her business interests and her channel partners, and promoting the interests of her son (whose name also appears in the building's inscription).

In examining Eumachia's building in Pompeii's Forum, the inscriptions on that building, and Eumachia's statue in that building, we demonstrated the importance of boldness, supporting your partners, creative thinking, knowing CA expenses, and the benefit of being a leader in your industry.

Customer Aquisition Strategies

These five Stage 1 customer acquisition lessons derived from Eumachia's actions are enumerated in Table 4.2:

Table 4.2. Summary of Chapter 3 Lessons

Lesson	Stage 1: Create Customer Attention
11	Be Bold
12	Support Your Channel Partners
13	Think Outside the Box
14	Attracting Customer Attention Is Costly
15	Be a Leader in Your Marketplace

CHAPTER 4

Scaurus

We now move to our third entrepreneur, Aulus Umbricius Scaurus (referred to in this text as Scaurus), his food products, and the customer acquisition techniques he used. Scaurus' products were at the other end of the spectrum from Eurysaces' socially exalted bread and the brilliant white togas made from Eumachia's wool. Scaurus produced a family of fish sauces, categorized under the term *garum*, in the mid-first century AD, and he is thought to have been alive when Mt. Vesuvius erupted in AD 79.[1]

Garum was most often used in cooking or as a condiment and was produced in many locales across the Roman Empire. Despite being vilified by aristocratic authors, garum was a favorite of the Roman people. See Appendix B for a recipe for making a modern version of a garum-like sauce.

Garum and Rome's Elite

Like bread and togas, garum was subject to comment by ancient Roman writers, but not with the soaring phrasemaking left us by Juvenal and Vergil. Instead, garum was criticized as mere putrefaction by the ancient encyclopedist Pliny the Elder.[2] Seneca the Younger (an advisor to the Emperor Nero) went even further and descriptively wrote that the fishy product "burns up the stomach with its salted putrefaction."[3]

Garum and Its Poet

Yet, garum, too, had a poet write of its "virtues." Garum's lasting taste on the palate was so malodorous that the ancient Roman poet Martial, whose first book of poems commemorated the opening of the Colosseum in Rome (in AD 80), wrote admiringly of a friend's virility that could stay intact even after his mistress consumed "half a pint of garum."[4]

Martial also left us an exquisitely colorful description of garum's scent when he listed garum among an inventory of horrendous stenches that included a chick rotting in an egg and a "billy goat fresh from his amours."[5] Martial elsewhere in one of his books admitted (like most Romans) to a "thirst(s) for noble garum"—although he confesses that he was drunk at the time.[6]

However, if the adage that one man's trash is another's treasure was ever true, it seems so in the case of garum. Despite his criticism of garum, Pliny the Elder reported that garum was also good for many medical conditions, including fresh burns,

dog bites, ulcers, and mouth and ear pain.[7] Pliny
also noted that six pints of said putrefaction, in
one particular instance, sold for 1,000 sesterces, or
nearly $4,000 today![8]

Garum Production

Pliny also reported that one noted center for
production of quality garum was Pompeii,[9] where,
as we have seen with Eumachia, Vesuvius destroyed
the city but preserved many elements of Pompeii's
daily business life. Among all the destruction in
Pompeii, significant traces of the once vibrant garum
industry remain, including much archeological
evidence of Scaurus' dominant role in that industry.
But before we begin our specific discussion of
Scaurus' customer acquisition techniques, let's first
look more closely at garum and its production.

Garum and Related Products

The process for making garum, although a bit
revolting to our modern tastes, was a fermentation
process. Garum's manufacturing took place far from
the city center, as it was not only malodorous, but
also needed to be near significant amounts of fish,
as fish were the main ingredient in the production
process.

According to Prof. R. I. Curtis, one of the leading
authorities on garum:

In general, Romans placed into a small vat particularly anchovies, sardines, and mackerel, and added salt at prescribed ratios and sometimes various herbs, spices, or wine. They used weights to press down on the concoction, covered it, and allowed it to remain in the sun for several months. At the end, they withdrew the liquid by using a basket, filtered it, and placed it in a terracotta transport vessel, or amphora.[10]

Figure 5.1 shows an amphora (amphorae, pl.) used in the packaging and transport of products such as garum and wine. Photo: Courtesy of Shutterstock

The garum produced in Pompeii was typically packaged and transported in a one-handled amphora called an *urceus* (Figure 5.2).[11]

Figure 5.2: Shows a large and a small urceus used in the local transport of garum in and around Pompeii. Notice the now faint painted inscription on upper portion of the larger vessel. Photo: Courtesy of Claus Ableiter, 2007.

Often, the urceus was painted with inscriptions that contained production-related information, as seen on the middle of the larger vessel in Figure 5.3.

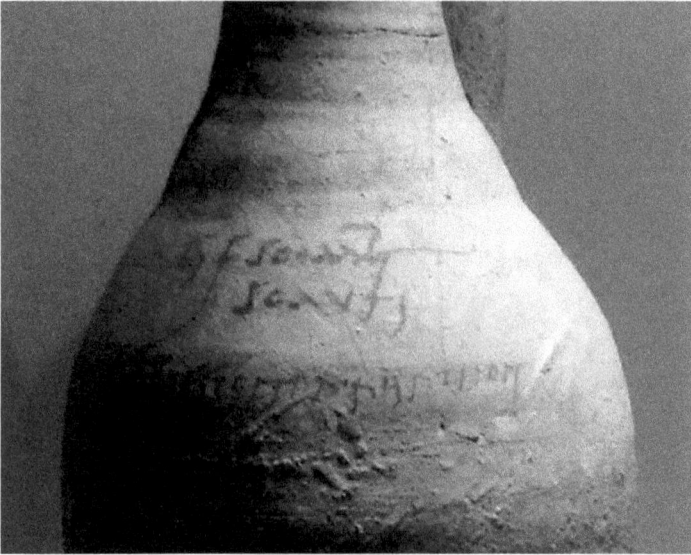

Figure 5.3. A close-up of the large urceus in Figure 5.2 shows the painted inscription from the upper portion of the larger vessel.[12] *Photo: Courtesy of Claus Ableiter, 2007.*

Varying Quality of Fish Sauce

The specific production process used and the timing of the garum's removal from the production vats yielded varying qualities of the liquid. Garum of premium quality was described by the word *flos*, meaning "the flower or best" (the term *fleur de sel*, or "flower of salt" is still used for a premium sea salt as seen in Figure 5.4).

Figure 5.4. A modern package of salt by the Artisan Salt Company containing the Fleur de Sel, the flower of salt. Photo: Robert Lerner.

Other lesser or second-quality fish sauces and process byproducts resulting from the garum production were called *liquamen, allec,* and *muria* and are ranked by quality in Table 5.1.[13]

Table 5.1. Garum and Its Products

Product	Description
Garum (flos)	Premium fish sauce
Garum	Fish sauce
Liquamen	Thought to be close to garum
Allec	Undissolved fish remnants of the process
Muria	Salty liquid byproduct of the process

Trade Information Painted on the Urcei

The inscriptions on the Pompeian urcei used in the garum trade are critical to our discussion of the product-focused second stage of the customer acquisition process. The information contained in the inscriptions, whether written out or abbreviated because of user familiarity, often contained one or more of the following bits of information shown in Table 5.2:[14]

Table 5.2. Urcei Descriptive Elements

Inscription	Information or Meaning
Name	To whom the container was sent
Shipper	Transporter of the container
Physical Details	Weight of the container
Contents	Type of fish ingredients, for example, mackerel
Content Qualifier	Quality, for example, flos, or aged
Producer/Owner	For example, Scaurus

The Flower of Garum

Curtis, in his studies of garum and its production, reports the most common elements of the fish-sauce container inscriptions were the words *garum* and *flos*. Curtis argues that *flos* was used so frequently, and even repeated as part of an inscription (for example, garum, the flower of the flower), that the word was transformed from merely technically informative into a method of *advertising and differentiating* one vendor's product from another.[15]

This approach can been seen in modern ad campaigns striving to emphasize the beneficial qualities of farm grown products by using such terms as farm fresh, healthy, GMO (genetically modified organism) Free, and organic, to differentiate one's company's produce from another (all contained in Figure 5.5).

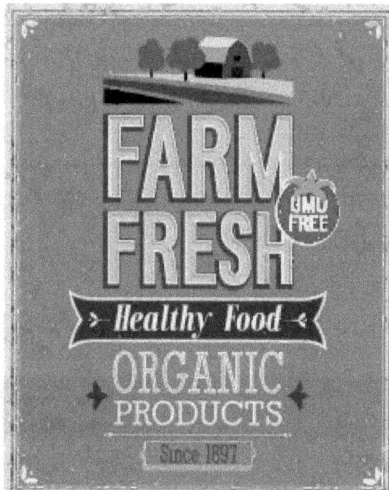

Figure 5.5. The use of various beneficial qualities in an ad. Image: Courtesy Shutterstock.

Curtis also notes that the second most used adjective on the garum containers after flos was the Latin word for best—*optimum*.[16] Whether optimum was superior to flos is less relevant here than that another adjective was used to describe, and most likely advertise, the vessel's contents. Additional product descriptors, in selected instances, also found their way into the inscriptions detailing the contents.

One example of the additional information was the fish that the garum was made from, for example, mackerel, and another was that the contents were aged. Thus, it was beneficial to the ancient garum producer to promote the most marketable characteristics of the product to the customer.[17] To show Scaurus' advertising touch, Curtis provides what is perhaps the gold standard in ancient fish-sauce container inscriptions:

> *the flower of garum, made from the mackerel, a product of Scaurus, from the shop of Agathopus.[18]*

This ancient label provided the consumer with the following five elements:[19]

Table 5.3. The Gold Standard in Garum Marketing Used by Scaurus.

Label Element	Description
1. The contents	Garum
2. The quality	Flower
3. The key ingredient	Mackerel
4. The owner/producer of the product	Scaurus
5. The distributor of the product	Agathopus

The information on the packaging of Scaurus' products rivals any product ingredient listings found on present-day food packaging. Such a comprehensive approach to product-focused Stage 2 customer acquisition by Scaurus provides our first of two lessons.

Lesson 16: Emphasize the Positive

Despite using *putrefaction* to describe garum, Pliny also described it as a "kind of choice liquor."[20] So, despite the many literary and social critiques of garum's attributes, Scaurus wisely chose to emphasize the product's "choice" liquor-like characteristics and to appeal to the discriminating ancient consumer with such terms as quality (flower of garum), ingredients (mackerel), and standing behind his brand by indicating his production company in the inscription.

Ogilvy and the Advertising of Food

David Ogilvy, when discussing advertising for the food industry, reminded advertisers to "build your advertisement around appetite appeal,"[21] and to "show the package."[22] Figure 5.6 is an example of an early ad that would surely meet Ogilvy's idea of an "appealing" food product ad despite its being for cod liver oil.

This advertisement dates from the 1890s, but note the smiling little girl standing behind the package. Notice how the packaging for this product, originally made by the fermentation of cod livers, contains positive words such as *palatable, digestible, nutritive, tonic, best* (on the side panel), and *finest* (like the flower of garum).

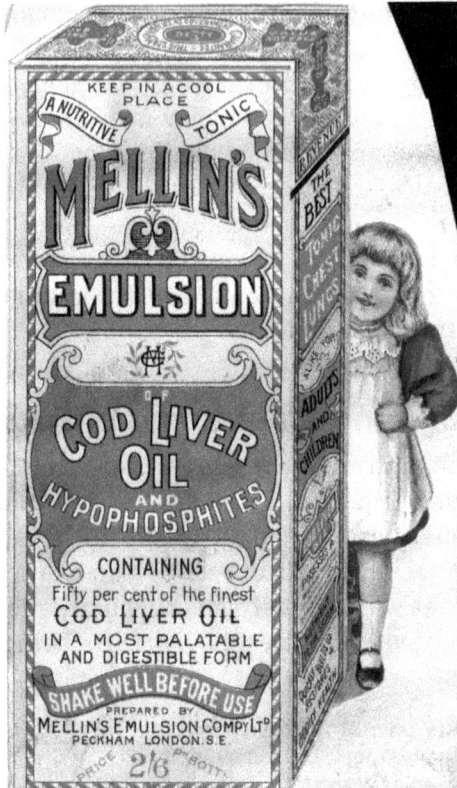

Figure 5.6. An "appealing" 1890s ad for cod liver oil. Image: Advertising Archive/ Courtesy of Everett Collection.

The Second Lesson from Scaurus' Inscriptions

Both *garum* and *flos* were sufficiently common that the words were often reduced to a "G" and an "F" as a shorthand.[23] This can be seen in an enlargement of part of the inscription on the urceus shown in Figure 5.2. The enlarged image (Figure 5.7) shows a G for *garum*, F for *flos*, and then the words **Scombri** (mackerel) and **Scavri** (Scaurus).[24]

124

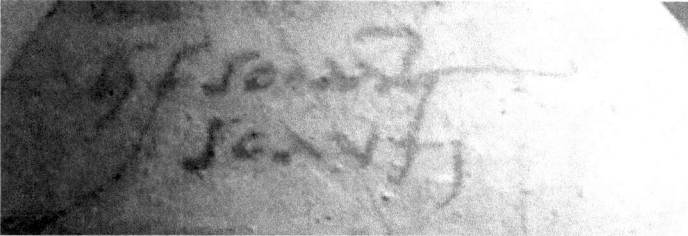

Figure 5.7. An enlargement of the inscription (CIL IV, 5692) on the urceus in Figure 5.2 with the G for garum and F for flos visible. The rest of this enlarged inscription indicates the garum is made from mackerel (Scombri) by Scaurus (Scavri).

Scaurus and other Pompeian fish-sauce producers likely knew their customers' tastes and sought to convey the key messages about their products on their containers. Even if Pompeian buyers were illiterate, they might still recognize the G or the F on the urcei (which was likely immediately recognized as a garum container, much as we recognize a wine bottle).[25]

Professor Curtis determined that the urcei Scaurus produced were those that typically offered the most descriptive inscriptions of the quality of garum contained in the vessels—to such an extent that Scaurus' name "must have been inextricably linked with Pompeian fish-sauce."[26] The second product-focused CA lesson we obtain from this effort by Scaurus to inform his customers about the product they purchased relates to the need to communicate with clarity.

Lesson 17: Be Descriptive

Of all the surviving urcei in Pompeii and Herculaneum (a town near Pompeii also destroyed by Mt. Vesuvius), a staggering 28.6% had—in one format or another—the name of Aulus Umbricius Scaurus,[27] or a family member, slave, his freedman (or one of his freedman's shops) as part of the inscription.[28]

Because urcei inscriptions varied widely across the spectrum of garum purveyors,[29] it is unlikely that government officials required all the descriptors used. Therefore, we must conclude that elements of Scaurus' descriptive information were important to the buyer and the buying decision. We cannot know, but perhaps Scaurus' dominance can be attributed to the consistent,[30] detailed, and descriptive product messages he provided on his urcei.

Ogilvy called this detailed product messaging "informative" advertising. In the second stage of the customer acquisition process, an advertiser must move beyond the generalities of gaining a potential customer's attention and quickly inform the prospect of the most important elements of the product or service to properly position the offering.

An excellent example of a modern food product positioned using descriptive keywords are the packaged sardines offered by Crown Prince in Figure 5.8. The adjectives on the package inform the consumer that the sardines are "skinless & boneless," "in olive oil," and a "natural source of Omega-3." Perhaps not much has changed in nearly 2,000 years of product advertising, for the potential buyer of the Crown Prince sardines can quickly learn the product's most salient characteristics from the packaging, just as a customer of Scaurus' garum could in ancient Pompeii.

Figure 5.8. The descriptive packaging for sardines that makes the contents attractive and visible to the buyer. Photo: Courtesy of istockphoto.com.

Scaurus' Home

Critical clues about Scaurus' business activities that survived the cataclysm of Vesuvius were elements of a floor mosaic found in his home. The house was identified as his because of the surviving floor mosaic. Scaurus had a mosaic constructed in the atrium, and near each corner was inlaid a mosaic of an inscribed urceus.

Three of these mosaic urcei contained Scaurus' name, just as it was inscribed on his garum containers. According to Curtis, this mosaic ". . . has no parallels anywhere in the Roman world."[31] Very much like Eurysaces and Eumachia, Scaurus spoke innovatively through stone in a way that remains a marvel.

127

Scaurus' Mosaic Inscriptions

The four extant inscriptions, as reported by Professor Curtis in his paper, "A Personalized Floor Mosaic from Pompeii," are contained in mosaic representations of the urcei that measure a bit more than two feet in height (Figure 5.9),[32] and Curtis dated to about AD 30.[33]

The four inscriptions, of which the image in Figure 5.9 is translated in a, can be read as follows (translations are from Curtis):[34]

> *a. The flower of garum, made of the mackerel, a product of Scaurus, from the shop of Scaurus*
>
> *b. The flower of Liquamen*
>
> *c. The flower of garum, made of the mackerel, a product of Scaurus*
>
> *d. The best liquamen, from the shop of Scaurus*

Figure 5.9. One of the four urcei mosaics found in Scaurus' home in Pompeii. [35] Photo: Courtesy of Claus Ableiter, 2007.

There can be little doubt that this was Scaurus' home and that he chose to decorate that home with the inscriptions he used on his vessels to package and transport his garum. Scaurus' devotion to his product and his business forms our next Stage 2 CA lesson.

Lesson 18: Display Your Passion for Your Product

Scaurus conducted business in his home, and he intended for his buyers to see his name and his commitment to his product. Scaurus likely believed in and was proud of his business, or he would not have displayed his name so prominently on the urcei, or in his home's atrium (the most public part of his home). The name Scaurus became inextricably linked with his product, creating a personal affiliation that testified to his commitment to his products and his business.

Is it any different today where many major companies place their founder's name on their products *and* their buildings? Just a few well-known examples include Ford, Elizabeth Arden, The Campbell Soup Company, Dell, and Trump (Figure 5.10).

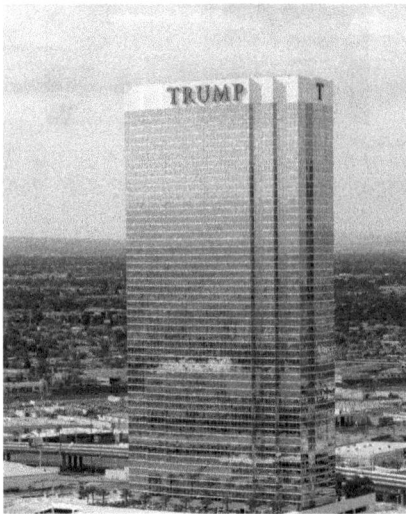

Figure 5.10. Trump International Hotel Las Vegas displaying the Trump name and a "T" on the building. Photo: Courtesy of Shutterstock.

Donald Trump places his name on his buildings—emphasizing for all to see that Trump promises premium quality and the opportunity to transact with a successful businessperson, just as Scaurus likely strove to accomplish with his floor mosaics.

Scaurus' Creation of a "Brand"

Beyond being passionate for his product, Scaurus, as we have seen, repeatedly placed his name on the vessels containing his product. Today, we call this product branding, and we see brand names on everything—the clothing we wear (Ralph Lauren), the food we eat (Purdue chicken), bedding we sleep under (Martha Stewart and Ralph Lauren), the cars we drive (Ford), and even the computers we use (Dell). We also have a plethora of well-known brands not based on their founders' names, such as Nike, GM, IBM, and Google.

The issue for successful customer acquisition is less the naming convention and more the support behind the brand. Successful branding today, besides a quality product, requires creativity, commitment, communications, consistency, and capital. From what we have seen so far of Scaurus, his "branding" efforts met these requirements and in so doing provide our next customer acquisition lesson.

Lesson 19: Create a Powerful Brand

A brand, as defined by the American Marketing Association, is a "name, term, design, symbol, or any other feature that identifies one seller's good or service as distinct from those of other sellers."[36] A quality brand is also one of the most valued assets a company can have. In many instances, the brand is the company.

David Ogilvy recognized the importance of creating a brand and reminded his advertisers to "include your brand name in your headline."[37] (Notice the prominence of the Hathaway brand name in the classic Ogilvy ad in Figure 1.9). Ogilvy pushed the branding concept even more aggressively for food-related products: "It is the total personality of the brand rather than any trivial product difference which decides its ultimate position in the market."[38]

Scaurus followed this approach as well and included his name, which seems his "brand," on his product's packaging to help communicate information on his product to the consumers of his garum. This ancient informational branding has been called *proto-branding* to distinguish it from more modern, image-centric branding (Figure 5.11).[39]

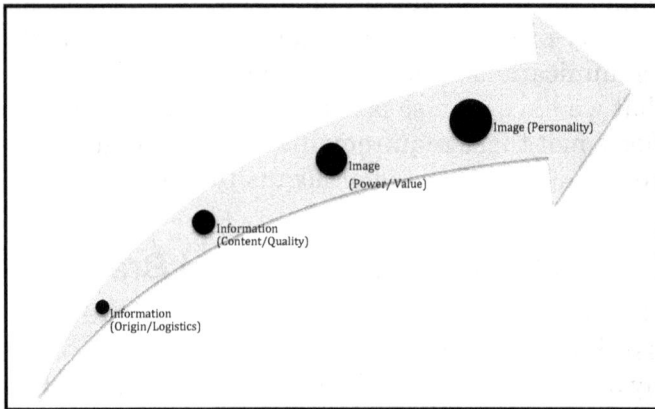

Figure 5.11. The evolution of branding from informational proto-branding in antiquity to the image-centric branding of the present day.[40] A brand today connotes the seller's personal commitment to their side of the customer acquisition transaction, and it has become a shorthand means of representing the quality and personality of both the item sold and the company doing the selling.

A modern example of using one's name to communicate power and personality in the luxury product marketplace is the perfume created by Donald Trump's daughter Ivanka. The product is prominently branded with the Trump name, and it strives to inform the consumer that the liquid in the container is superior to its competition (Figure 5.12). Note, also, the tagline "Strength in Grace and Beauty" on the lower left intended to help further define the product and refine the brand.

Figure 5.12. Shows the Trump name prominently displayed on the bottle of Ivanka Trump perfume and the signage. Photo: Courtesy of Shutterstock.

Brand Equity

As we have seen, the Trump brand is instantly recognizable and known to connote premier quality. The brand's strength adds value to Trump's products and services. This added value, called *brand equity*, is "reflected in how consumers think, feel, and act with respect to the brand and the prices, market share, and profitability the brand commands for the firm."[41] Specific advantages of strong brand equity include:[42]

1. Improved perception of product performance

2. Greater consumer loyalty

3. Less vulnerability to competitive marketing actions

4. Less vulnerability to marketing crisis

5. Larger margins

6. More inelastic consumer response to price increases

7. More elastic consumer response to price decreases

It is perhaps helpful to think of a brand's value-add "as the premium the consumer would pay for a branded product or service, compared to an identical unbranded version of the same product/service."[43] Additional profit can be mined from a powerful brand as well demonstrated by Trump, and even from a proto-brand, as shown by Scaurus' success with his garum's labeling.

Scaurus and His Employment Practices

Scaurus' name (and brand) was not the only name found on his garum packaging. At least one female member of the family worked in the business with both female and male former slaves of Scaurus.

Scaurus' willingness to employ men *and* women, both free and slave, in his business enterprise shows his entrepreneurial genius extended well beyond marketing and into his employment practices. We know of his use of a heterogeneous workforce because names of a freeborn female (Umbricia, possibly a daughter or his wife), a freedwoman (Umbricia Fortunata), and freedmen (Umbricius Agathopus, as seen in Figure 5.3, and A. Umbricius Abascantus) have been found on his containers.[44] Scaurus' documented use (such evidence from antiquity is rare) of his mixed gender workforce provides our final customer acquisition lesson in this chapter:

Lesson 20: Seek Talent Wherever It Is Found

Although it was a common practice in ancient Rome to use one's slaves and former slaves in business, it is much rarer to find documented use of freeborn women, and in Scaurus' case, that practice was memorialized on his garum containers for all to see.

David Ogilvy, whose advice we have sought throughout this text, was also determined to hire the top talent available in his time.[45] Ogilvy followed an interesting ritual whenever a person was placed in charge of an Ogilvy & Mather office. Ogilvy sent the new office manager a matryoshka doll from

Gorky, Russia. When the executive finished opening each successively smaller doll, he found a note from Ogilvy that said, "If each of us hires people who are smaller than we are, we shall become a company of *dwarfs*. But if each of us hires people who are bigger than we are, Ogilvy & Mather shall become a company of *giants*."[46] To successfully execute one's customer acquisition goals, like a Scaurus or an Ogilvy, one should seek the best talent wherever it might be found.

Chapter Summary

In this chapter, we saw that Scaurus created a successful business empire based on fish fermentation by offering what we must assume were quality products, informing his customers with extensive packaging labeling, and employing talented staff. In the process, Scaurus showed us how to create a successful product marketing campaign and the importance of establishing a powerful product brand (Stage 2 of the customer acquisition process as seen in Figure 5.13).

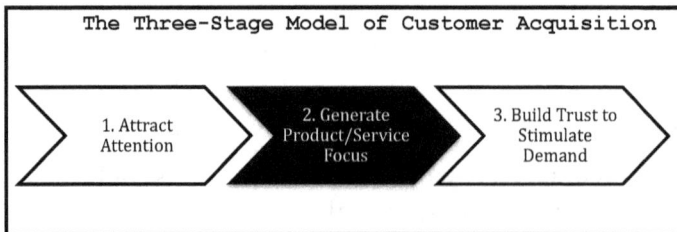

The Three-Stage Model of Customer Acquisition

1. Attract Attention

2. Generate Product/Service Focus

3. Build Trust to Stimulate Demand

Figure 5.13. The second stage of customer acquisition discussed in this chapter. Scaurus' management of his garum business showed methods for generating consumer interest in his product (no matter how malodorous).

The five lessons we formed from Scaurus'
Stage 2 customer acquisition actions involving the
generation of product/service-focused advertising are
enumerated in Table 5.4.

Table 5.4. Summary of Chapter 4 Lessons

Lesson	Stage 2: Generate Product/Service Focus
16	Emphasize the Positive
17	Be Descriptive
18	Display Your Passion for Your Product
19	Create a Powerful Brand
20	Seek Talent Wherever It Is Found

CHAPTER 5

Atticus

We have seen that bread production financed Eurysaces' tomb, wool helped pay for Eumachia's building in Pompeii's Forum, and the manufacture of garum funded Scaurus' home. We will now study the activities of our fourth entrepreneur Atticus, an aristocratic banker whose "product" was credit, as much "the lifeblood of business" today[1] as in antiquity.

Figure 6.1. A modern copy of an ancient Roman bust of Cicero,[2] Atticus' lifelong friend, confidant, and banking client.

Atticus was born into a wealthy equestrian family in 109 BC. Cicero was his schoolmate, lifelong friend, and banking client. Cicero, as we saw earlier, decried the vulgarity of work, but he was comfortable using Atticus' services, in one case, to settle a large debt to Julius Caesar.[3] Atticus' other clients included Marcus Brutus, Mark Antony's wife (Fulvia), and the government of Athens and the ancient Greek city of Sicyon.

Atticus was no ordinary banker, for Atticus was an aristocrat of excellent family lines back to early Rome's ancient kings, of extraordinary wealth, with connections that encompassed many of Rome's best families, and Atticus, later in life, had the stature associated with being the leading equestrian of his time.

Figure 6.2. Bust of Atticus' client Marcus Brutus.[4]

Atticus was no ex-slave like Eurysaces or provincial manufacturer like Scaurus, and Eumachia's elite status in provincial Pompeii could not begin to rival that of Atticus. But despite his great wealth and stature, we have no tomb or statue of Atticus, nor any other physical legacy of the man to enlighten us about his entrepreneurial activities.

However, in Atticus' case, we have something in many ways far more informative than stone monuments—we have his biography, a treasure trove of information that can be mined for details of Atticus' business activities. The operative word here is **mined**. Because, as we have seen, the elite disdained labor and laborers, Atticus' legacy is only lightly sprinkled with business-related references, but those references exist, and they can be used to extract lessons of the customer acquisition techniques this long-surviving aristocrat used.

Atticus' Biography

Atticus' biography that has come down to us was written before his death, sometime between 35 and 32 BC.[5] A second edition of the biography was reissued after his death in 32 BC, between 32 and 27 BC.[6] Atticus' biography is unique for two reasons:

1. It is the only Roman biography coming down to us that was written while the subject was living.

2. It is the only surviving biography we have of the life of an ancient businessperson.

The biography was written because Atticus, besides his banking activities, was an author of a

Roman history and was, therefore, included in an ancient biographical work discussing great Latin historians. Thus, the biography contains even fewer snippets of his business interests than might otherwise have been included. Those business interests of Atticus encompassed real estate, a troop of gladiators, publishing, and finance.

Before we move to the biography, we must understand that the times in which Atticus lived were some of ancient Rome's most unsettled and dangerous. Atticus lived through the Roman Republic's collapse and the Roman Empire's bloody birth. He survived three civil wars, Julius Caesar's dictatorship and assassination, and the splitting of the empire between Caesar's adopted son Octavian and Caesar's deputy Mark Antony. Ultimately, Octavian won sole power and ruled Rome as its first emperor (and wearer of homespun clothing), Augustus Caesar.

A timeline of Atticus' life is presented in Table 6.1 and a brief overview of the people listed on that timeline is provided in Table 6.2. (For a much fuller discussion of Atticus' life and business approach, please see *Career Turbulence, Ancient Lessons for Survival in the Modern Workplace* by this author).

Customer Aquisition Strategies

Table 6.1. Timeline of Atticus' Life

Date (BC)	Event	Age of Atticus
109	Birth of Atticus	Born
106	Birth of Cicero	3
100	Birth of Caesar	9
88–82	Sulla's Civil War	21–27
86/85	Death of Atticus' father Atticus leaves Rome for Athens	23/24
65	Atticus returns to Rome	44
63	Cicero elected consul (Roman Republic's highest office)	46
60	Republic controlled by Caesar, Crassus, and Pompey the Great (The First Triumvirate)	49
58	Cicero exiled	51
57	Cicero's return from exile Atticus inherits 10M sesterces (about $40M)	52
56	Atticus marries Pilia	53
53	Crassus killed in Parthia	56
49	Caesar's Civil War begins	60
48	Caesar victorious Caesar named dictator by Roman Senate	61
44	Caesar assassinated Conspiracy led by Brutus and Cassius Caesar in his will adopts his grand-nephew, Octavian Civil war again erupts Death of Atticus' wife	65
43	Cicero executed	66
42	Octavian and Antony join forces and defeat Brutus and Cassius	67
37	Atticus' daughter marries Octavian's leading general, Agrippa	72
32	Death of Atticus	77

Table 6.2. Ancient Romans Listed in Table 6.1

Name (DOB–DOD)	Description
Agrippa (c. 64/63 BC–12 BC)	Leading commander of Octavian's forces; married Atticus' daughter and, later, Octavian's daughter
Antony (83 BC–30 BC)	Served under Caesar; consul in 44 BC; combined with Octavian to defeat Brutus and Cassius; ordered Cicero's execution; with Octavian's collaboration, seized control of the Republic; later defeated by Octavian in another civil war
Brutus (85 BC–42 BC)	Leading conspirator, with Cassius, in Caesar's assassination; Atticus' friend
Cassius (c. 85 BC–42 BC)	Leading conspirator, with Brutus, in Caesar's assassination
Caesar (100 BC–44 BC)	Consul, 59 BC; triumvir with Pompey and Crassus; dictator, 49 BC–44 BC; assassinated on March 15, 44 BC
Cicero (106 BC–43 BC)	Consul 63 BC, author, politician, lawyer, orator, Atticus' lifelong friend, executed in 43 BC
Crassus (115 BC–53 BC)	Richest man in Rome, consul in 70 BC and 55 BC, triumvir with Caesar and Pompey
Octavian (63 BC–AD 14)	Julius Caesar's grandnephew, adopted as Caesar's son and heir through his will, combined forces with Mark Antony and seized control of the Republic, later defeated Antony and became the Emperor Augustus
Pilia (c. 75 BC–44 BC)	Atticus' wife
Pompey (106 BC–48 BC)	Consul, 70 BC, 55 BC, and 52 BC; triumvir with Caesar and Crassus; defeated by Caesar during civil war
Sulla (c. 138 BC–78 BC)	Consul 88 BC and 82 BC, dictator 82–81 BC

Atticus' Life (109–65 BC)

Atticus was born into an aristocratic family, and his father died when he was in his early twenties. From his father, Atticus inherited 2 million sesterces (or nearly $8M today). To avoid being caught up in the first of the three civil wars, Atticus, in 86 BC when he was twenty-three, removed himself to Athens and stayed there for nearly two decades. Cicero briefly visited Atticus in Athens in 79 BC,[7] and Atticus occasionally traveled to Rome over the intervening years. In 65 BC, Atticus finally returned to Rome full time, when another schoolmate became consul, the Roman Republic's highest elected office.

Atticus' Life (64–44 BC)

Atticus' close friend Cicero became consul in 63 BC but suffered the fate of exile in 58 BC for alienating the major powerbrokers of the time (Caesar, Pompey the Great, and Crassus, then the richest man in Rome). Atticus supported Cicero financially while he was in exile, and he was pleased to welcome Cicero back after his return from exile in 57 BC. In 58 BC, Atticus inherited 10 million sesterces (nearly $40 million today) from an uncle.

Atticus, during all the turmoil that swirled around Cicero and the Republic, managed to stay on good terms with the major political factions jockeying for control of the state. Ultimately, civil war erupted in 49 BC. Julius Caesar decisively defeated his adversaries, and the Senate appointed him Dictator of the Roman Republic in 48 BC.

Atticus' Life (47–43 BC)

Atticus managed to stay friendly with Caesar's allies and the faction that would comprise the core of the conspiracy that murdered Caesar for his perceived monarchial aspirations on the Ides (15th) of March in 44 BC. Following the dictator's assassination, power was in flux, and a third civil war broke out.

Cicero, at this time, tried desperately to restore the Republic's stability and publicly condemned Mark Antony's tyrannical ambitions in a series of speeches (*The Philippics*), but when Antony managed to consolidate sufficient power (in league with Caesar's adopted son Octavian), Antony demanded Cicero's execution (43 BC).

Cicero was beheaded at his villa outside Rome, and his head and hands (that wrote *The Philippics*) were sent to Mark Antony in Rome. Antony's wife Fulvia (to whom Atticus had provided support and financial aid) abused Cicero's head before it was publicly displayed in the Roman Forum where Cicero had first achieved his fame as a lawyer and orator.

Figure 6.3. A statue of Cicero currently in front of the Italian Palace of Justice in Rome. Photo: Robert Lerner.

Figure 6.4. Mark Antony's wife gleefully abusing the head of Atticus' good friend Cicero with her hairpins in a painting by Pavel Svedomsky. Fulvia received financial support from Atticus following Caesar's murder. [8]

Atticus' Life (42–32 BC)

Atticus lived for another decade after Cicero's death and stayed on good terms with Mark Antony and Octavian as they jointly ruled the Roman Empire. Mark Antony was the matchmaker for the marriage of Atticus' daughter to Agrippa, Octavian's second in command.

Figure 6.5. A bust of Atticus' son-in-law Marcus Vipsanius Agrippa. Photo: Robert Lerner.

Before he died in 32 BC, Atticus managed to betroth his granddaughter to Tiberius Caesar (who became the emperor that appointed Pontius Pilate governor of Judea), a testimony to the esteem in which Atticus was held.

Atticus' Biographer

Atticus' biographer, Cornelius Nepos, was an equestrian like Atticus.[9] Nepos was ten years younger than Atticus was but lived through the same tumultuous events as his subject. Nepos was a prolific writer of books on famous politicians, generals, and historians (hence, his rationale for Atticus' biography).

Nepos was linked with Atticus beyond being his biographer. He said that a book he wrote on Caesar's adversary Cato the Younger was written ". . . at the urgent request of Titus Pomponius Atticus."[10] Additionally, Nepos dedicated his work entitled *Great Generals of Foreign Nations* to Atticus. Nepos also informed us in his biography of Atticus: ". . . because of our intimacy I was often familiar with the details of his (Atticus') domestic life."[11] Nepos was an intimate friend and admirer of Atticus and most likely not an unbiased source.

Given Nepos' personal relationship with Atticus and that Atticus was living when Nepos' biography was first published, we can reasonably assume that, before publication, Atticus reviewed and approved the biography. Atticus might also have contributed to the work by sharing letters or information with Nepos. Therefore, Nepos' portrayal of his subject and his subject's time were likely a version of events not necessarily as they occurred, but as Atticus wanted them portrayed.

Still, we must ask why Atticus agreed to a biography at a late stage of his life (he was in his mid-sixties). An obvious reason might be that Atticus was honored by his friend's effort to list him among Rome's great historians. However, a more likely rationale for the biography is that the work would provide an opportunity for an intimate to write a friendly history of Atticus' survival during the Roman Republic's bloody fall, one that would highlight the good deeds Atticus performed during the trauma resulting from the Roman Republic's collapse.

Whatever the catalyst for Nepos writing a friendly biography of Atticus, the result reflected positively on Atticus' legacy, and thus, it greatly benefited Atticus as he reached for still higher levels for himself and his descendants in Rome's highly stratified society. This effort by Atticus to ensure a reputation for integrity brings us to our first lesson of Stage 3 customer acquisition. Remember that in Stage 3 CA, we look for the establishment of an exchange that recurs and does not end after one purchase. Without trust in a relationship, there will not be ongoing purchases, and trust requires a partner with a reputation for integrity. Anything less undermines a relationship.

Lesson 21: Build Relationships on a Foundation of Trust

If Atticus had been perceived as or portrayed as unscrupulous, he would have been unsuccessful in establishing ongoing business relationships with Rome's elite. Similarly, if a company's product or service fails to live up to the expectations set by its advertising (CA Stage 1) or product marketing (CA Stage 2), then all effort expended in gaining a customer will be lost. That is not to say that an initial transaction will not occur, but the goal here is to have sales repeat and increase over time.

Donald Trump wisely reminds us that not every businessperson is ethical and emphasizes a burden on the buyer as well as the seller. Trump bluntly advises, "If you are stupid and gullible, it is only a matter of time before someone takes your money."[12] If someone takes your money, you will hopefully not look to repeat a transaction with that business "partner."

All this seems at odds with Ogilvy's earlier assertion that "the consumer isn't a moron," but Ogilvy was speaking of how to communicate with an audience, and Trump reminds us that, individually, not everyone is trustworthy—on either side of the transaction. Remember that our goal here is to work to establish a relationship that sustains repeatable transactions and that those who deal with you must trust you (and you them).

Nepos Extols Atticus' Virtues

Throughout Atticus' biography, Nepos describes his subject as a superman, extolling Atticus' wisdom, refinement, culture, sense of duty, loyalty, dignity, foresight, natural goodness, amiability, independent judgment, goodheartedness, generosity, and even his unfailing memory. Atticus selected the correct biographer for the job if he wanted to ensure that his image was unblemished.

Partly because of his fawning approach to his subject, his language, and many factual errors, some modern historians have commented negatively on Nepos' abilities as an historian and as a biographer. Others, recognizing the complex time in which Nepos wrote, downplay Nepos' shortcomings and praise his commitment to the dying Roman Republic.

Thus, we have a range of judgments on Nepos and his works. Those judgments range from Nepos being called an "intellectual pygmy"[13] to his being lauded as an important ". . . commentator on his times (that) has been underappreciated."[14]

Regardless of modern opinion, Atticus' wise decision to select Nepos as his biographer, or more appropriately his "PR flack," forms our next lesson in Stage 3 customer acquisition.

Lesson 22: Image Management Requires Micromanagement

The key here for us is that Nepos had what Atticus or anyone else might wish for in a friendly biographer—impeccable credentials combined with more than a touch of credulity. Atticus must have been comfortable with Nepos writing the biography, or he would have stopped the effort early in the process. Perhaps Atticus was all that Nepos wrote he was; however, when protecting or enhancing one's image, especially a brand image, nothing can be taken for granted. Atticus, as an author himself, knew that a miscommunication could have undermined all the effort he spent building his reputation in the first place.

Even when you retain the best marketing or advertising people money can buy, you must stay as involved in the campaign as feasible. Looking to Donald Trump, an acknowledged leader in brand creation and brand management, we find he advises, "Get the best people, and don't trust them."[15] Again, the term **trust** rears its head—and, as Trump says, even when fully trusting, do not stray too far from the action.

Nepos on Atticus' Business Approach

Nepos, in his biography, unsurprisingly spoke little about Atticus' business interests. He, however, described how Atticus worked with the ancient Athenians to provide loans.[16] Nepos informs us that when Athens ". . . needed to negotiate a loan and could not do so on fair terms, he (Atticus) always came to the rescue, and in such a way that he never exacted from them excessive interest, nor would he allow them to remain in debt beyond the stipulated time. And both these conditions were to their advantage, since he did not by indulgence allow their debt to grow old, nor yet increase by the piling up of interest."[17]

The lesson obtained in this instance from Nepos' positive rendition of Atticus' dealings with his Athenian clients is that the recruitment (and retention) of your customers requires transactional fairness. The critical aspect of any relationship (and Atticus' relationship with the Athenians spanned decades) is the perception of fairness between parties—buyer and seller (or, as in Atticus' case, creditor and debtor). The need for fairness in an ongoing relationship complements this chapter's first lesson (Lesson 21) dealing with trust and forms this chapter's third CA lesson.

Lesson 23: Customer Acquisition Requires Transactional Fairness

We see that Atticus was fair in his dealings and knew that the timely repayment of debts was an obligation to be lived up to even by a government. That he dealt over decades with Athens' financial needs indicates the power of Atticus and his fairness. That willingness to be fair, despite his power, should be acknowledged, and Atticus' expectation that debts were to be repaid according to the agreement's terms was reasonable.

Reasonable and fair are descriptors that every seller or service provider should seek to attain because, together, these terms describe the partner you want in an ongoing relationship. After all, unfairness and unreasonableness are not wanted in any partner at any time. Donald Trump also commented on the importance of fidelity from all involved parties in commercial transactions, when he advised unequivocally, "Your word is golden."[18] With customers, it is always best to say as you intend to do and do at least as much as you say. Atticus' Generosity

Nepos informs us of one additional dimension of Atticus' banking relationship with the Athenians. Nepos reports that Atticus provided the Athenians ". . . another act of generosity; for he made a distribution of grain to the entire people . . . ."[19]

This donation was not small, and given the political sensitivity of grain (as we saw earlier in our discussion of the politics of bread), not surprisingly, the good deed came to the attention of Atticus' friend Cicero. Cicero wrote in a letter to Atticus, ". . . what's all this? *Panem populo* (bread for the people) at Athens? Do you think that is in order?"[20]

Cicero questioned the grain donation's propriety and asked whether it was a bribe (as we saw Augustus comment on in chapter 1). Cicero, in that letter, answered his question by saying, "Not that my volumes have anything against it, since it was not a largesse (a bribe) to fellow countrymen but a piece of generosity to foreign hosts."[21]

Given that the donation was to foreigners (non-Romans), it was not a political payoff on Atticus' part, but Cicero's jab hinted that Atticus' gift to the Athenian people skirted being a bribe. However, the donation's benefit was clear—the Athenians lionized Atticus and even erected statues to Atticus and his wife in Athens.[22] Atticus' demonstrated generosity establishes our fourth Stage 3 customer acquisition lesson.

Lesson 24: Give Back

The Athenians greatly appreciated Atticus' donation, and he likely reaped a positive impact on his relationship with his clients. With any donation, whether public or private, the most important motivation should always be to benefit those in need. A donor's underlying rationale (such as in Atticus' case) need not be disclosed, but hopefully, the gift is made from a generosity of spirit, for by the act of giving, the donor benefits.

It has been reported "that people who give more charitably are 43% more likely to say they are 'very happy' than nongivers."[23] Donald Trump makes this point when he argues, "To keep momentum going, you must have intrinsic values as well as monetary values, and you must recognize when it is time to start giving back."[24]

Nepos Tells Us More about Atticus' Attributes

Besides Atticus' many saintly attributes enumerated above, Nepos used four critical phrases to describe Atticus that I want to focus on because of their direct relevance to a businessperson's striving for the establishment of strong and ongoing customer relationships. The phrases Nepos used are that Atticus:

1. "Never lied, nor could he tolerate falsehood"[25]

2. "Avoided the suspicion of wrong-doing"[26]

3. "Had a spirit of economy"[27]

4. Was "gracious to the humble and on an equality with the great."[28]

We see that Nepos presented Atticus to his readers as the ideal man (which perhaps the "gracious" Atticus encouraged). He was the perfect business partner, as he was scrupulously honest and conservative in handling money.

Additionally, we see from Nepos that Atticus was gracious to those less fortunate than he and, as important, in a position to deal on equal footing with the great and powerful—exactly what you want in your choice of a banker—a sensitive person who can go head to head with the powerful on your behalf. The successful positioning of Atticus as the ideal partner provides us with this chapter's final customer acquisition lesson.

Lesson 25: Understand What the Customer Desires in a Partner

Given Nepos' well-constructed panegyric to Atticus, we are left asking, who would not want to do business with this man? Atticus made it easy to choose him as a trustworthy banker and a reliable friend. The presentation of a company and its owner as the optimal partner for a buyer, as Nepos did for Atticus, is a key to obtaining and retaining a business relationship. Perhaps an effective means to emphasize the importance of this point is with an example in the negative. As an alternative to Nepos' "good" Atticus, look at the "bad" Richard Nixon as he was depicted in a poster used by Democrats in the 1960 presidential election (Figure 6.6).

Figure 6.6. An updated Democratic poster of Vice President Richard Nixon used during the Kennedy-Nixon 1960 election. Nixon lost to Kennedy, but just eight years later, Nixon was elected the 37th President of the United States. Nixon became the first President to resign from the office in disgrace in 1974. Photo: Courtesy of the Granger Collection.

Nixon lost to John F. Kennedy in that election but managed over the next few years to successfully rebrand his image and win the White House in 1968. However, the makeover was only skin-deep, for Nixon resigned in disgrace in 1974.

Chapter Conclusion

In this chapter, we used Atticus and his biography as a model for the development of our Stage 3 customer acquisition lessons. Atticus, through Nepos, was positioned as the ideal man and partner, demonstrating the importance of building a trusted persona and brand integrity to ensure repetitive customer exchanges.

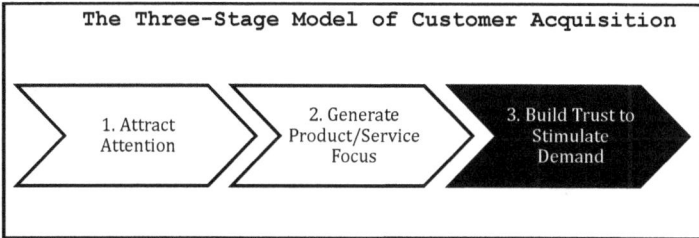

Figure 6.7. Highlights the third and final stage of customer acquisition discussed in this chapter. Atticus' efforts to develop a positive experience with his financial clients testify to the importance of trust in creating ongoing customer relationships.

The five lessons we formed in this chapter all revolved around Atticus' efforts to ensure his peers, and posterity saw him as a man of integrity, fairness, and generosity.

Table 6.3. Summary of Chapter 5 Lessons

Lesson	Stage 3: Generate Product/Service Focus
21	Build Relationships on a Foundation of Trust
22	Image Management Requires Micromanagement
23	Customer Acquisition Requires Transactional Fairness
24	Give Back
25	Understand What the Customer Desires in a Partner

CHAPTER 6

Concluding Lessons

We have studied four ancient Roman entrepreneurs as they presented themselves to their audiences. Let's take one final look at each, not as he or she created his or her images and wished to be perceived, but through the alternative lenses of history available to us.

Atticus

When we last left Atticus, we could only admire the flawless image provided us by Atticus and his biographer Cornelius Nepos. Nepos reported that Atticus was unblemished, the ideal citizen, loyal friend, and honest financier. So, we must ask, was Atticus as flawless as Nepos would have us believe? If we briefly turn to our other source of information on Atticus, his close friend Cicero, we see a somewhat different picture of the man emerge.

The Atticus discernible from Cicero's letters is a man able to brutally and frankly assess both Cicero's and Atticus' times (the collapse of the Roman Republic) and the political challenges they faced (surviving the resultant turmoil and bloodshed). The Atticus Cicero reveals is a far cagier person than the one Nepos presents to his readers. Atticus, interestingly, maintained a corpus of Cicero's letters to him, but not one of Atticus' letters to Cicero was ever published.

Cicero Labels Atticus a "Political Animal"

In letters written to Atticus in 56 and 55 BC, when Caesar, Pompey the Great, and Crassus held sway in Rome, Cicero wrote, "You are a political animal by nature,"[1] and, "As for your admonition to behave like a politique (a political moderate) and to keep to the inner row (a place of safety in an ancient board game), I shall do so."[2] Cicero knew his friend to be more chameleonic than Nepos would have us believe of his subject who could "tolerate no falsehood."

Atticus and the City of Sicyon

There is an insight into Atticus' business practices in Cicero's letters that refines our view of that generous banker to the Athenians. In six separate missives to Atticus written from January 61 BC to July 59 BC,[3] Cicero describes Atticus' attempts to use him to procure repayment of a loan from the ancient Greek city of Sicyon.

Cicero was so familiar and frustrated with Atticus' demands for assistance in obtaining repayment of the overdue loan that Cicero labeled Atticus' efforts "the siege of Sicyon."[4] Cicero never intimates whether Atticus was successful in collecting the debt, but his letters ceased any mention of Sicyon after the July 59 BC epistle.

However, the ancient author Pliny the Elder, nearly a century after Atticus' death, wrote of Sicyon that it ". . . was for a long period a native place of painting. But all the pictures there had been sold to meet a debt of the community, and were removed from ownership of the state to Rome. . . ."[5] Pliny does not state to whom the paintings went to settle the debt, but he provided a date when the loan finally settled—56 BC.

Perhaps it was just coincidental, and we cannot be certain that Atticus received the settlement, as other loans might have been outstanding, but the timing is interesting. Additionally, in all the letters discussing Sicyon's debt repayment, Cicero surprisingly never mentions any other competing interests demanding a debt collection.

Atticus and the Ides of March

There is one last item in our discussion of Atticus' "political nature." In Dr. Alice Hill Byrne's doctoral thesis completed in 1920, she noted the importance of the well-respected Atticus authoring a text on the family history of Marcus Brutus, lead conspirator in Julius Caesar's assassination.

Atticus, in his genealogy of Brutus' family, connected by descent his close friend Marcus Brutus to an ancient Roman hero and regicide, Marcus Junius Brutus. Junius Brutus freed the Romans from the rule of kings (by murdering the reigning king) and, in so doing, helped create the Roman Republic.

Atticus' public and authoritative linkage of the two Brutuses might have helped pressure Marcus Brutus into taking his deadly course against Julius Caesar on the Ides of March. Brutus celebrated his bloody act, depicted in Figure 7.1, by minting a coin to commemorate the day (Figure 7.2). The coin remains one of the most famous coins ever minted.

Thus, the genteel Atticus might very well have "influenced the career of Brutus and the course of history by bringing the connection (between the Marcus and Junius Brutus) into new prominence in the public mind."[6] Quite an achievement, potentially altering history's course—not bad for a man who could tolerate neither falsehood nor the suspicion of wrongdoing! Below the surface, there was perhaps more than a bit of Richard Nixon in Atticus.

Figure 7.1. An 1804/5 painting by Vincenzo Camuccini of the murder of Julius Caesar on March 15, 44 BC.[7]

Figure 7.2. The coin Brutus had minted with two daggers and the date to celebrate Caesar's assassination on the Ides of March. The cap of liberty between the daggers was traditionally given to slaves after their manumission, and it was included on the coin to symbolize the freedom gained by the Roman people. Brutus' portrait was stamped on the obverse side of the coin. [8]

A Final Lesson from Atticus

I provide these examples of Atticus' behavior to show that although Nepos presented Atticus as the ideal man, reality might have been much less so. And we now gain a much clearer perspective about why Atticus might have wanted his biography written. Atticus understood that perception of his earlier life could constrain his children's future under the reign of Caesar's descendants. Atticus seems never to have confused the reality of his actions with the myth he wished to leave behind, and this wisdom provides our final customer acquisition lesson from Atticus.

Lesson 26: Never Fall Prey to Your Image-Making

Atticus was determined to leave posterity an image of his making to benefit both his legacy and his progeny. It is often said that the victors write history,[9] and Atticus outlived all his enemies and most of his friends, so he, too, could have his history written unimpeded.

The core lesson we learned earlier from Atticus was the importance of integrity in the customer acquisition process, but here we have a complementary lesson—a lesson that reminds us that the seller's marketed image and reality should always be aligned as closely as possible. If the two begin to diverge, work diligently to keep them proximate, and if you cannot, always make sure that you are fully aware of their distance apart.

Scaurus

We saw earlier that Scaurus was a successful marketer of his fishy products and controlled nearly 30% of the Pompeian market for garum. A garum container with the name of Scaurus inscribed on it has been found as far from Pompeii as the mouth of the Rhone River, near Arles in southern France.[10]

Scaurus created a sophisticated and profitable enterprise. And Scaurus, much like Eurysaces, would have wanted to highlight his occupational success to testify to his importance in class-sensitive Pompeian society. Scaurus accomplished this, not just by placing his name on his urcei, but also by creating his mosaic urcei, which he used to advertise his "business, his wealth, and most of all Scaurus himself."[11]

Professor Curtis reminds us that this display was not just unique; the elite would also have looked down on it as something "one might expect from the a member of the nouveaux riches, eager to boast of his newly found wealth . . . ."[12]

The Elite's Opinion of Tradesmen

To create a retail business of the scope of Scaurus' in ancient Rome, at least according to Cicero, retailers "would get no profits without a great deal of downright lying . . . ."[13] Cicero adds that the "least respectable of all are those trades which cater for sensual pleasures," such as fishmongers, butchers, poulterers, perfumers, dancers, and anglers. Given Cicero mentioned fish-related trades twice, we must assume that Cicero and his peers would have accused those of the garum trade in general, and Scaurus in particular, of being vulgar and disingenuous.

A Scaurus, possibly our entrepreneurial Scaurus, appears in Petronius' novel *The Satyricon*. Petronius, to further re-enforce the buffoonery of the ex-slave Trimalchio (whom, as we saw earlier, has been linked by many to Eurysaces), has Trimalchio brag that he is honored to have Scaurus as a regular houseguest.

The aristocrats would have heartily laughed at anyone bragging about a processor of fish guts as an important guest. The elite sought every opportunity to denigrate someone like Scaurus. Scaurus might not have had all the servile limitations of the ex-slave Eurysaces, but his chosen profession retained an odor Roman society's upper crust disdained, even while they devoured his garum.

Scaurus' Determination

We, however, know more about Scaurus' determination to succeed than just what can be found on his fish-sauce containers. Though Pompeii was destroyed, additional surviving elements (beyond all the urcei and his home) include his family's tomb and its funerary inscription (see Figure 7.3). The tomb demonstrates the wealth Scaurus accumulated from his garum business, for the tomb is one of the larger found in Pompeii.[14] A surviving inscription on the tomb reads:[15]

To the memory of Aulus Umbricius Scaurus, son of Aulus, of the tribe of Menenia, duumvir with judiciary authority. The city council voted the place for a monument to this man and two thousand sesterces toward the cost of the funeral; that voted also that an equestrian statue in his honor should be set up in the Forum. Scaurus the father to the memory of his son.

Let's analyze the inscription. Scaurus the son was named the same as his father and predeceased his father (hence, the inscription's last sentence). Scaurus' son was one of the town's two chief magistrates (duumvir), and he had judicial authority for the area. The town council voted 2,000 sesterces (about $8,000 today) for the younger Scaurus' funeral (which likely included gladiatorial games), provided the site for the tomb, and paid for the construction of a statue in the town center (he probably died while in office).

Figure 7.3. An 1817 engraving by Charles Heath of the tomb of Scaurus' family that was first unearthed in 1812. The images on the tomb likely represent the gladiatorial games held as part of the funeral of the younger Scaurus. Image: Courtesy of istockphoto.

Scaurus, the skillful entrepreneur, most likely used the wealth he built on a foundation of decomposing fish to buy his son into a powerful governmental position and to establish his family as respected and visible members of the Pompeian community. Our final CA lesson from Scaurus is drawn from his determination to raise his family's status.

Lesson 27: Sometimes, You Have to Throw Money at a Problem

There are times when good intentions alone will not suffice. The discrimination Scaurus endured, regardless of his financial success, never dissipated, and Scaurus would have been well aware of his status. However, he chose to ignore his business' critics and created a successful enterprise that allowed him to buy some respectability, at least in local (Pompeian) circles, for himself and his family in general and his son in particular.

This is not an argument to do what Scaurus did, but to think like Scaurus. In other words, do not be afraid to invest capital in growth or as an indicator of your success to further your success. Scaurus operated in a different time, in a different place, under different rules. But the lesson applies.

Donald Trump, who has more than his share of critics and like Scaurus is not shy about visibility or throwing his money around, importantly notes one additional benefit of maintaining a high profile. Trump declares, "There has always been a display of wealth and always will be . . . a display is a good thing. It shows people that you can be successful."[16] There is an old saying about how money cannot buy love or friends, but money can buy "a better class of enemy."[17]

Eumachia

In chapter 3, we learned that Eumachia constructed a magnificent building in Pompeii's Forum. However, Eumachia's building was not her only construction. Archeologists have also unearthed another edifice commissioned by Eumachia—her tomb (Figure 7.4).

Figure 7.4. Eumachia's tomb as it stands today in Pompeii. Note the semicircular structure (a bench) in the center of the tomb complex. Photo: Courtesy of Scala/Art Resource, NY.

Eumachia built the tomb for her son, her household, and herself. The tomb's size is larger than that of Scaurus. The tomb is the largest found to date in Pompeii—nearly 46 feet long and more than 42 feet wide.[18] The tomb's perimeter is more than three times larger than that of Eurysaces! Additionally, Eumachia's tomb featured a large semicircular seat for viewers to sit and contemplate the deceased.

Was Eumachia Overreaching?

However, an ancient wall sealed off the bench so it was inaccessible to the tomb's visitors. Professor Michael Scott in his text, *Space and Society in the Greek and Roman Worlds*, speculates that the seat was "not sanctioned by the city council,"[19] and likely, Eumachia was not entitled to build such a seat into her tomb.

Scott also notes one more important point about Eumachia's tomb. Eumachia's tomb was not long hers. "By the mid-first century AD it was being used by another family, that of Cn. Alleius Nigidus,"[20] who was possibly a freedwoman's son.[21]

Although wealthy, Alleius Nigidus commissioned no public or commercial buildings for Pompeii's people. But Nigidus, despite his lineage, still achieved great popularity among the locals because of his sponsorship of spectacular gladiatorial games. One surviving Pompeian notice of the games reads:

> *Thirty pairs of gladiators furnished by Cn. Alleius Nigidus Maius, quinquennial duumvir [five-yr magistrate elected about 55 AD], together with their substitutes [for those killed], will fight at Pompeii November 24, 25, 26. There will be a hunt. Hurrah for Maius the quinquennial!"[22]*

A Final Lesson Drawn from Eumachia's Tomb

What lesson can be drawn from these two ancient data points—Eumachia's tomb seat blocked by the city council and the tomb reused by another family? And if the family that used Eumachia's tomb was somehow linked to Eumachia, that linkage likely transpired **after** Eumachia passed from the scene, when she was hardly in a position to protest. From two events that occurred after Eumachia's death, we could extrapolate a powerful lesson from what Eumachia endured after her death.

Lesson 28: The Memory of Friends Is Shorter than that of Enemies

Eumachia's achievements are all the more outstanding when we remember the discrimination she faced both as a woman and as a businesswoman in ancient Rome. We can only imagine that along the way, she stepped on more than a few toes and made powerful enemies.

It would be no surprise that, after she died, those who most resented her success and were too intimidated to act while she was alive wasted no time in diminishing her accomplishments. Perhaps her grandiose, but unsanctioned, tomb was the chosen means to strike back at Eumachia, inflicting in death what none could manage in her lifetime.

Eumachia's tomb, unlike that of Scaurus (and other men in Pompeii),[23] makes no mention of a publicly financed funeral, statue, or monument. The simple but telling inscription on Eumachia's tomb reads:

> *Eumachia, daughter of Lucius,*
> *[built this]*
> *for herself and her family.*[24]

For all Eumachia did for Pompeii's citizens, one might have expected more from the town council to commemorate Eumachia's life. This CA lesson then is a reminder not to tread lightly, but be aware that all actions have consequences, often unintended consequences. Those consequences, both intended and unintended, should be evaluated as thoroughly as possible before boldly embarking on and along your chosen path.

Eurysaces

As mentioned at this text's outset, as far as Eurysaces is personally concerned, our only source of information on the man is his tomb. However, I would like to share a description of the working conditions at an ancient Roman flourmill operating in the mid-second century AD, nearly two centuries after Eurysaces' death. Although taken from a work of fiction,[25] this "glimpse of hell,"[26] should not be dismissed as mere literary invention by the author.

Lucius Apuleius, the author, was born in about AD 125 in the Roman province of North Africa (modern Algeria), traveled widely around the empire including a visit to Rome, and died about AD 180. Here is his depiction of the suffering slaves grinding flour at the mill:

> *O good Lord, what a sort of poor slaves*
> *were there; some had their skin bruised all*
> *over black and blue, some had their backs*
> *striped with lashes and were but covered*
> *rather than clothed with torn rags, some*
> *had their members only hidden by a*
> *narrow cloth, all wore such ragged clouts*
> *that you might perceive through them all*
> *their naked bodies, some were marked*
> *and burned in the forehead with hot irons,*
> *some had their hair half clipped, some*
> *had shackles on their legs, ugly and evil*
> *favored, some could scarce see, their eyes*
> *and faces were so black and dim with*
> *smoke, their eyelids all cankered with*
> *the darkness of that reeking place, half*
> *blind and sprinkled black and white with*
> *dirty flour like boxers which fight together*
> *befouled with sand.*[27]

And of the animals also used at the mill, the author writes:

> *They had their necks all wounded and worn away with old sores, they rattled their nostrils with a continual cough, their sides were bare with continued rubbing of their harnesses and great travail, their ribs were broken and the bones did show with perpetual beating, their hoofs were battered very broad with endless walking, and their whole skin ragged by reason of mange and their great age.*[28]

Eurysaces' Labor Practices

Did Eurysaces own mills with working conditions similar to those depicted by Apuleius? We do not know, but as discussed early in this text, the baking business was the province of slaves and ex-slaves, and there is perhaps no clearer evidence of slave involvement in the baking business than an inscription left on a carbonized loaf of bread found in Pompeii (Figure 7.5).

The inscription was made by a bread stamp, and by the first century AD, if a loaf of bread was purchased commercially or made available by the state, it was likely marked with a bread stamp.[29] Such a stamp would have contained trade information similar to that found on Scaurus' urcei. Stamps or seals were also used for inscriptions on bricks,[30] tiles, pipes, and lamps as protection against potential fraud or theft.[31]

Figure 7.5. A preserved, carbonized loaf of bread from Pompeii with the inscription left from a bread stamp still visible. Image: Courtesy of the Picture Collection, the New York Public Library, Astor, Lenox and Tilden Foundations.

The translated inscription on the loaf in Figure 7.5 reads, "Made by Celer, slave of Quintus Granius Verus."[32] The bread of the slave Celer is but one example, but we can assume that slave labor was probably very much a part of Eurysaces' baking business and comprised much of the workforce depicted on his tomb (Figure 7.6).

Figure 7.6. Laborers, likely slaves, depicted on Eurysaces' tomb. Photo: Robert Lerner.

We do know with greater certainty, however, that Eurysaces used animals in bread making. This can be seen in the detailed images from his tomb (Figures 7.7 and 7.8).

Figure 7.7. What seems to be a mule used in the milling process depicted on Eurysaces' tomb. Photo: Robert Lerner.

Figure 7.8. A horse used with the kneading machine depicted on Eurysaces' tomb. Photo: Robert Lerner.

Water-Powered Mills

Vitruvius, an architect and writer who lived in the same century as Eurysaces, informed us that water-powered mills were also used in ancient Rome. A modern model of such a water-powered grain mill, based on Vitruvius' description, is shown in Figure 7.9.

Figure 7.9. A modern model of an ancient water mill, based on the description of such a machine from the writings of the ancient Roman architect Vitruvius.[33]

We cannot determine whether Eurysaces used water-powered mills in his bread production, but if he had, we think he would have proudly represented them on his monument, as he displayed men, animals, and other aspects of the baking business.

In many ways, Eurysaces' tomb was a work of beauty, but the slave-based labor structure that likely underpinned its operation, though accepted by ancient Roman society, is repulsive to our modern senses.

Modern Labor Practices

Today, more than 2,000 years after Eurysaces died, we see many products we purchase produced in sweatshops that greatly resemble ancient Rome's mills described by Apuleius. Sweatshops can be found in Bangladesh (912 workers killed in a building collapse on April 24, 2013),[34] Pakistan (289 workers killed in factory fire on September 12, 2012),[35] and India (with its rampant child labor).[36]

These so-called modern businesses, where children and adults risk their health and their lives for just a few pennies a day, make products for us with even less intrinsic value than Eurysaces' bread. They are also reminders that the world has changed little from Eurysaces' time.

Perhaps we should not set our expectations of Eurysaces' labor practices too high, but we should set the bar for today's businesspeople and consumers of their products—as high as necessary to spare the lives and health of any factory workers in any location.

A Final Lesson from Eurysaces' Tomb

We cannot infer from Eurysaces' friezes whether he lacked concern for his slaves, and so we cannot separate the images presented to us by Eurysaces and those of Apuleius. However, this in no way inhibits our ability to formulate our final, modern customer acquisition lesson.

Lesson 29: Forgo Unjust Business Practices

If unfair or unjust practices support your profits, eventually, you will pay a high price, of which the customer loss will only be a small part. Unfortunately, profit, too, often trumps people, and modern advertising techniques seem ever more able to smother that reality.[37]

Eurysaces the ex-slave might have managed to overcome many inequalities found in ancient Roman society, but if you search for repeatable business transactions and customer retention, do not use ignorance or corporate structure to excuse unsavory employment practices.

Chapter Conclusion

In this chapter, when we looked closely at our chosen role models, we saw another side to the actions of Atticus, Scaurus, and Eumachia, and the underbelly of Eurysaces' industry, the baking business. The Widow Bates' ulterior motives were clear for all to see—a mourning young widow with her eyes set more firmly on the future than the past.

With our four entrepreneurs, any underlying motives were much more difficult to discern because the passing centuries obscured much, and in their cases, secrets were literally taken to the grave. However, despite the challenges, we constructed four concluding, albeit hard-edged, customer acquisition lessons from examining the darker shadings of these four ancient businesspeople or their business interests (Table 7.1).

Table 7.1. Concluding Customer Acquisition Lessons

Lesson	Concluding Customer Acquisition Lessons
26	Never Fall Prey to Your Image-Making
27	Sometimes, You Have to Throw Money at a Problem
28	The Memory of Friends Is Shorter than that of Enemies
29	Forgo Unjust Business Practices

Immutability of Our Ancient Lessons

Early in this text, we saw that the Widow Bates and her use of one of the limited media of communication available to her in 1800 was the model on which this text was conceived. And although the twenty-nine lessons in customer acquisition we formulated were based on the marketing and promotional efforts of Eurysaces, Scaurus, Eumachia, and Atticus operating nearly two millennia before the mourning widow Bates, they can be applied across today's broad spectrum of communication vehicles.

The lessons we have seen as insensitive to the passage of time are also effectively medium independent. Regardless of the communication vehicle or vehicles used to gain the attention and retention of customers, the lessons will comfortably overlay our selected media alternatives—from stone tombs to digital media. Here are the twenty-nine immutable lessons from Eurysaces, Eumachia, Scaurus, and Atticus, with the three stages of customer acquisition, one last time:

Stage 1: Attract Attention (Eurysaces)

- Lesson 1: Plan Thoroughly
- Lesson 2: Seek Separation from the Pack
- Lesson 3: Alter the Familiar for Impact
- Lesson 4: Repetition Builds Absorption
- Lesson 5: Provide the Facts
- Lesson 6: Leverage Testimonials
- Lesson 7: Assault the Consumer's Senses
- Lesson 8: Engage a Viewer with Humor
- Lesson 9: Outrage Garners Attention
- Lesson 10: Ensure Message Consistency

Stage 1: Attract Attention (Eumachia)

- Lesson 11: Be Bold
- Lesson 12: Support Your Channel Partners_
- Lesson 13: Think Outside the Box
- Lesson 14: Attracting Customer Attention Is Costly
- Lesson 15: Be a Leader in Your Marketplace

Stage 2: Generate Product/Service Interest (Scaurus)

- Lesson 16: Emphasize the Positive
- Lesson 17: Be Descriptive
- Lesson 18: Display Your Passion for Your Product
- Lesson 19: Create a Powerful Brand
- Lesson 20: Seek Talent Wherever It Is Found

Stage 3: Build Trust to Stimulate Demand (Atticus)

- Lesson 21: Build Relationships on a Foundation of Trust
- Lesson 22: Image Management Requires Micromanagement
- Lesson 23: Customer Acquisition Requires Transactional Fairness
- Lesson 24: Give Back
- Lesson 25: Understand What the Customer Desires in a Partner

Concluding Lessons

- Lesson 26: Never Fall Prey to Your Image-Making
- Lesson 27: Sometimes, You Have to Throw Money at a Problem
- Lesson 28: The Memory of Friends Is Shorter than that of Enemies
- Lesson 29: Forgo Unjust Business Practices

The Three-Stage Model of Customer Acquisition

1. Attract Attention (Eurysaces & Eumachia)

2. Generate Product/Service Interest (Scaurus)

3. Build Trust to Stimulate Ongoing Demand (Atticus)

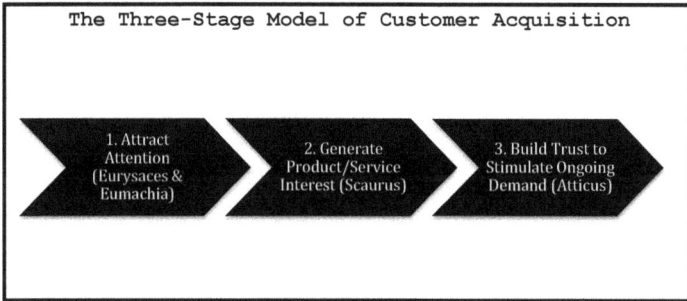

Figure 7.10. The three stages of customer acquisition.

Trimalchio's Tomb

Trimalchio's Tomb Construction Instructions

In Petronius' *The Satyricon*, Trimalchio, while hosting an extravagant dinner party, issues instructions for his tomb's design to his drunken stone carver. Selected parts of the instructions, which would have created a tomb of imperial dimensions (more than 100 feet long and 200 feet deep), include:[1]

> *First, of course, I want a statue of myself. Around it I want an orchard with every known variety of fruit tree. You'd better throw in a vineyard too.*
>
> *Also, I want you to carve me several ships with all with sail crowded . . . .*

(One of Trimalchio's occupations was shipping, but this depiction dramatically diverges from the usual funeral depiction of a final journey incorporating ships without sail.[2])

> *On my right I statue of Fortunata*
> *with a dove in her hand.*

(Trimalchio's wife also was a former slave and chorus girl, perhaps to be depicted on the tomb as the goddess Venus.[3])

> *And in the middle stick a sundial so that*
> *anyone who wants the time of day will*
> *have to read my name.*

(Ensures interaction with the tomb's audience and possibly alludes to a great sundial the Emperor Augustus constructed in Rome.)

Trimalchio's Epitaph

Petronius has Trimalchio further instruct his intoxicated stonemason to carve a long and self-serving epitaph, elements of which are the following:

> *HERE LIES*
>
> *GAIUS POMPEIUS TRIMALCHIO MAECENAEUS,*

(Petronius sarcastically highlights Trimalchio's "great" name and lineage harking back to Pompey the Great and Gaius Maecenas, a friend and cultural advisor to the Emperor Augustus.)

> . . .
>
> *PIOUS AND COURAGEOUS,*
>
> *A LOYAL FRIEND,*
>
> *HE DIED A MILLIONAIRE,*
>
> *THOUGH HE STARTED LIFE WITH NOTHING.*

(Reminds all readers that despite his great wealth, Trimalchio had servile origins.)

> *LET IT BE SAID TO HIS ETERNAL CREDIT*
>
> *THAT HE NEVER LISTENED TO PHILOSOPHERS.*

(Perhaps a gibe at Nero's mother who advised Nero as a youth to avoid philosophy because she thought it unhelpful to a future ruler,[4] or the gibe was aimed at Nero's counselor Seneca.[5])

> *PEACE TO HIM.*
>
> *FAREWELL.*

Typically, the funerary inscription and the monument on which it was inscribed offered a unique opportunity for a slave or ex-slave on the margin of society to claim some status, even if

it was only achieved in death. With the fictional
Trimalchio and all the wealthy ex-slaves he was
intended to represent, Petronius parodied that effort
unmercifully.

A Modern Recipe for a Garum-like Sauce

Ingredients:

One quart of grape juice

Two tablespoons of anchovy paste

A pinch of oregano

Over medium heat, reduce grape juice until it thickens (about one-tenth of its original volume). Remove from heat, and stir in two tablespoons of anchovy paste. Add a pinch of oregano.[1]

Bibliography

Ancient Sources

Apuleius. *The Golden Ass.* Translated by William Adlington. Hertfordshire: Wadsworth Editions Limited, 1996.

Cicero. *In Catilinam.* Vols. 1–4. Translated by C. MacDonald. Cambridge: Harvard University Press, 1977.

—*Letters to Atticus.* Vols. 1–4. Translated by D. R. Shackleton Bailey. Cambridge: Harvard University Press, 1999.

—*On Duties.* Translated by Walter Miller. Cambridge: Harvard University Press, 2005.

Horace. *Satires and Epistles, Persius: Satires.* Translated by Niall Rudd. London: The Penguin Group, 1979.

Juvenal. *Satires.* Translated by Susanna Morton Braund. Cambridge: Harvard University Press, 2004.

Martial. *Epigrams.* Vols. 2–3. Translated by D. R. Shackleton Bailey. Cambridge: Harvard University Press, 1993.

Nepos. *On Historians.* Translated by J. C. Rolfe. Cambridge: Harvard University Press, 2005.

Petronius. *The Satyricon.* Translated by William Arrowsmith. New York: The Penguin Group, 1994.

Pliny the Elder. *Natural History.* Vol. 8. Translated by W. H. S. Jones. Cambridge: Harvard University Press, 2000.

—*Natural History.* Vols. 3 and 9. Translated by H. Rackham. Cambridge: Harvard University Press, 2005.

Plutarch. *Lives.* Translated by Aubrey Stewart and George Long. London: George Bell & Sons, 1894. Project Gutenberg. http://www.gutenberg.org/files/14033/14033-h/14033-h.htm

Suetonius. *Augustus and Nero.* Vols. 1–2. Translated by J. C. Rolfe. Cambridge: Harvard University Press, 2001.

Tacitus. *The Agricola and the Germania.* Translated by H. Mattingly. London: Penguin Books, 1970.

Virgil. *The Aeneid.* Translated by Edward McCrorie. Ann Arbor: The University of Michigan Press, 1995.

Vitruvius. *On Architecture.* Vols. 1–2. Translated by Frank Granger. Cambridge: Harvard University Press, 1998.

Secondary Sources

Andreau, J. *Banking and Business in the Roman World.* Cambridge: Cambridge University Press, 1999.

[2] Applegate, Ed (ed.). *The Ad Men and Women: A Biographical Dictionary of Advertising.* Westport: Greenwood Press, 1994.

Berdowski, Piotr (Rzeszow). "Roman Businesswomen. 1: The case of the producers and distributors of garum in Pompeii." *Analecta Archaeologica Ressoviensia,* (2008): 251–269.

Betts, Richard. *The Essential Scratch & Sniff Guide to Becoming a Wine Expert.* New York: Rux Martin/Houghton Mifflin Publishing Company, 2013.

Biel, Alexander L. "Converting Image into Equity," in *Brand Equity & Advertising,* edited by Aaker, David A. and Alexander L. Biel. Hillsdale: Lawrence Erlbaum Associates, Publishers, 1993.

Bodel, John, ed. *Epigraphic Evidence, Ancient History from Inscriptions.* London: Rutledge, 2001.

—*Roman Brick Stamps in the Kelsey Museum.* Ann Arbor: The University of Michigan Press, 1983.

Bonsall, Thomas E. *Disaster in Dearborn: The Story of the Edsel.* Stanford: Stanford University Press, 2002.

Brandt, Olle. "Recent Research on the Tomb of Eurysaces," *Opuscula Romana* 19, no. 2, (1993).

Burlingham, Bo and George Gendron. "The Entrepreneur of the Decade, An Interview with Steve Jobs, Inc.'s Entrepreneur of the Decade." *Inc.com,* (1989). http://www.inc.com/magazine/19890401/5602.html. Accessed September 24, 2013.

Byrne, Alice Hill. *Titus Pomponius Atticus: Chapters of a Biography.* Lexington: Bibliolife, LLC, 2009.

Carroll, Maureen. *Spirits of the Dead, Roman Funerary Commemoration in Western Europe.* Oxford: Oxford University Press, 2006.

Collins, Douglas. *America's Favorite Food: The Story of Campbell Soup Company.* New York: Harry N. Abrams, 1994.

Cooley, Alison E. and M. G. L. Cooley. *Pompeii and Herculaneum: A Sourcebook.* London: Routledge, 2014.

Courtney, Edward. *A Companion to Petronius.* Oxford: Oxford University Press, 2003.

Crossley, James G. *The Date of Mark's Gospel.* London: Bloomsbury T&T Clark International, 2004.

Curtis, Robert I. "A Personalized Floor Mosaic from Pompeii." *American Journal of Archeology.* 88, no. 4, (1984):557–566.

—"Product Identification and Advertising on Roman Commercial Amphorae." *Ancient Society* 15–17, (1984–6):209–228.

—"Umami and the Foods of Classical Antiquity." *American Journal of Clinical Nutrition,* doi: 10.3945/ajcn.2009.27462C 90, no. 3, (2009):712S–718S.

Davies, Penelope, J. E. *Death and the Emperor.* Austin: University of Texas Press, 2004.

Dixon, Suzanne. *Reading Roman Women.* London: Duckworth, 2003.

Dobbins, John J. and Pedar W. Foss, ed. *The World of Pompeii.* New York: Routledge, 2007.

Dunbabin, Katherine M. D. *Mosaics of the Greek and Roman World.* Cambridge: Cambridge University Press, 1999.

Duncan-Jones, R. P. "Review of the Wool Trade of Ancient Pompeii by Walter O. Moeller." *The Classical Review*, New Series 29, no. 1 (1979):190–191.

—*The Economy of the Roman Empire, Quantitative Studies*. Cambridge: Cambridge University Press, 1982.

Erdkamp, Paul. *The Grain Market in the Roman Empire: A social, political and economic study*. Cambridge: Cambridge University Press, 2005.

Fantham, Elaine, Helen Peet Foley, Natalie Boyem Kampen, Sarah B. Pomeroy, and H. Alan Shapiro. *Women in the Classical World*. New York: Oxford University Press, 1994.

Favro, Diane. *The Urban Image of Augustan Rome*. Cambridge: Cambridge University Press, 2008.

Forbis, Elizabeth. "Women's Public Image in Italian Honorary Inscriptions." *American Journal of Philology* 111, no. 4, (1990):493–512.

Frankl, Joseph H. "Whose Forum? Imperial and Elite Patronage in the Forum of Pompeii." *Studies in Mediterranean Antiquity and Classics* 3, no. 1, Article 3, (2013).

Galavarius, George. *Bread and the Liturgy: The Symbolism of the Early Christian and Byzantine Bread Stamps*. Madison: The University of Wisconsin Press, 1970.

Giacose, Ilaria Gozzini. *A Taste of Ancient Rome.*
Chicago: The University of Chicago Press,
1994.

Gruen, Erich S. *The Last Generation of the Roman
Republic.* Berkeley: University of
California Press, 1995.

Harris, W. V., ed. "The Inscribed Economy: Production
and distribution in the Roman empire in
the light of instrumentum domesticum."
Journal of Roman Archeology,
Supplementary Series 6, (1993).

Harrison, S. J., ed. *Oxford Readings in the Roman
Novel.* Oxford: Oxford University Press,
1999.

Harvey, Brian K. *Roman Lives, Ancient Roman
Lives as Illustrated by Latin Inscriptions.*
Newburyport: Focus Publishing, 2004.

Hays, Constance L. "David Ogilvy, 88, Father of
Soft Sell in Advertising, Dies," *New
York Times,* July 22, 1999. Accessed
September 22, 2012. http://www.nytimes.
com/1999/07/22/business/david-ogilvy-
88-father-of-soft-sell-in-advertising-dies.
html?pagewanted=all&src=pm

Hill, H. *The Roman Middle Class in the Republican
Period.* Westport: Greenwood Press, 1974.

Hingley, Richard. *Globalizing Roman Culture,
Unity, Diversity and empire.* New York:
Routledge, 2010.

Holliday, Peter J., ed. *Narrative and Event in Ancient Art*. Cambridge: Cambridge University Press, 1993.

Hope, Valerie M. and Janet Huskinson, eds. *Memory and Mourning: Studies on Roman Death*. Oxford: Oxbow Books, 2011.

Horsfall, Nicholas. "Prose and Mime." *Latin Literature*. Edited by Kenney, E. J. and W. V. Clausen. Cambridge University Press, 1982. *Cambridge Histories Online*, 290–293.

Imseng, Dominik. *Think Small: The Story of the World's Greatest Ad*. Full Stop Press, 2011.

Isaacson, Walter. *Steve Jobs*. New York: Simon & Schuster, 2011.

Jacob, H. E. *Six Thousand Years of Bread*. New York: Skyhorse Publishing, 2007.

Jones, A. H. M. "The Cloth Industry under the Roman Empire." *The Economic History Review*, Second Series 13, no. 2, (1960):183–192.

Jones, David. *The Bankers of Puteoli: Finance, Trade and Industry in the Roman World*. Gloucestershire: Tempus Publishing Limited, 2006.

Joshel, Sandra. *Work, Identity, and Legal Status at Rome: A Study of Occupational Inscriptions*. Norman: University of Oklahoma Press, 1992.

Keppie, Lawrence. *Understanding Roman Inscriptions*. Baltimore: The John Hopkins University Press, 1991.

Kotler, Philip, Kevin Lane Keller, and Peggy H. Cunningham. *Marketing Management*. Canadian 12th ed. Toronto: Pearson Prentice Hall, 2006.

Kurlansky, Mark. *Salt: A World History*. New York: The Penguin Group, 2003.

Lannon, Judie. "Asking the Right Questions: What Do People Do with Advertising?" in *Brand Equity & Advertising*. Edited by Aaker, David A. and Alexander L.Biel. Hillsdale: Lawrence Erlbaum Associates, 1993.

Laurence, Ray. *Roman Pompeii*. London: Rutledge, 1994.

Lerner, Robert. *Career Turbulence: Ancient Lessons for Survival in the Modern Workplace*. Oshawa: Multi-Media Publications, 2014.

—*Entrepreneurship and Ethics in Ancient Rome: The Management Lessons of Pliny the Younger*. Oshawa: Multi-Media Publications, 2013. A Note on Petr. Sat. 7.19–7.10." *Acta Ant. Hung* 45, (2005): 85–90. Accessed September 19, 2013. *Academia.edu*. http://www.academia.edu/942701/Under_Full_Sail_Trimalchios_Way_into_Eternity._A_Note_on_Petr._Sat._71.9-10).

Lewis, Richard, W. *Absolut Book, The Absolut Vodka Advertising Story*. Boston: Journey Editions, 1996.

Mann, Thomas C. and Green, Janet. *Over Their Dead Bodies Yankee Epitaphs & History.* Brattleboro: The Stephen Greene Press, 1962.

Mau, August. Trans. Francis Willey Kelsey. *Pompeii: Its Life and Art.* New York: The Macmillan Company, 1899.

Messaris, Paul. *Visual Persuasion, The Role of Images in Advertising.* Thousand Oaks: SAGE Publications, Inc, 1997.

More, Karl & Reid, Susan. *The birth of brand: 4000 years of branding.* Business History, 50:4 (2008), 419-432.

Moreley, Neville. *Trade in Classical Antiquity.* Cambridge: Cambridge University Press, 2007.

Moeller, Walter. "The Building of Eumachia: A Reconsideration." *American Journal of Archeology*, Vol. 76, No.3 (July, 1972), pages 323-327.

Moeller, Walter, O. *The Wool Trade of Ancient Pompeii. Studies of the Dutch Archeological & Historical Society.* Leiden: E. J. Brill, 1976.

Ogilvy, David. *Ogilvy on Advertising.* New York: Vintage Books, 1985.

Ogilvy, David. *Confession of an Advertising Man.* Harpenden: Southbank Publishing, 2011.

Osgood, Josiah. *Caesar's Legacy, Civil War and the Emergence of the Roman Empire.* New York: Cambridge University Press, 2006.

Owen, Stewart. "The Lando ImagePower Survey: A Global Assessment of Brand Strength." In Aaker, David A. and Biel, Alexander L., (eds.) *Brand Equity & Advertising.* Hillsdale: Lawrence Erlbaum Associates, Publishers, 1993.

Packard, Vance. *The Hidden Persuaders.* Brooklyn: Ig Publishing, 2007.

Petersen, Lauren Hackworth. "The baker, his tomb, his wife, and her breadbasket: the monument of Eurysaces in Rome." *The Art Bulletin* Vol. 85, No.2. (Jun., 2003), pp. 230-257. College Art Association. AccessMyLibrary (http//www.accesmylibrary.com). Accessed January 4, 2010.

Petersen, Lauren Hackworth. *The Freedman in Roman Art and Art History.* Cambridge: Cambridge University Press, 2011.

Petrovic, Andrej. "Under Full Sail: Trimalchio's Way to Eternity. A Note on Petr. Sat. 7.19-7.10." *Acta Ant. Hung.* 45, 2005, 85-90. Academia.edu. (http://www.academia.edu/942701/Under_Full_Sail_Trimalchios_Way_into_Eternity._A_Note_on_Petr._Sat._71.9-10). Accessed September 19, 2013.

Plaskin, Glen. "Playboy Interview: Donald Trump," *Playboy* 37, no. 3, (1990).

Prag, Jonathan and Ian Repath. *Petronius: A Handbook*. West Sussex: Wiley-Blackwell, 2009.

Raaflaub, Kurt A. and Mark Toher, ed. *Between Republic and Empire, Interpretations of Augustus and His Principate*. Berkeley: University of California Press, 1993.

Richmond, Ian A. *The City Wall of Imperial Rome*. Yardley: Westholme Publishing, 2013.

Ries, Eric. *The Lean Startup*. New York: Random House, Inc, 2011.

Roman, Kenneth. *The King of Madison Avenue: David Ogilvy and the Making of Modern Advertising*. New York: Palgrave Macmillan, 2009.

Rowsome, Frank, Jr. *Think Small: The Story of Those Volkswagen Ads*. New York: Ballantine Books, 1970.

Rubel, William. *Bread: A Global History*. London: Reaktion Books, 2001.

Scheidel, Walter and Sitta Von Reden, eds. *The Ancient Economy*. New York: Routledge, 2002.

Scott, Michael. *Space and Society in the Greek and Roman Worlds*. Cambridge: Cambridge University Press, 2012.

Shelton, Jo-Ann. *As The Romans Did*. New York: Oxford University Press, 1998.

—*The Women of Pliny's Letters*. New York: Routledge, 2013.

Smith, Andrew F. *Pure Ketchup: A History of America's National Condiment*. Columbia: University of South Carolina Press, 1996.

Stambaugh, John H. *The Ancient Roman City*. Baltimore: John Hopkins University Press, 1998.

Stem, Rex. *The Political Biographies of Cornelius Nepos*. Ann Arbor: The University of Michigan Press, 2012.

Stewart, Peter. *Statues in Roman Society*. Oxford: Oxford University Press, 2003.

Toynbee, J. M. C. *Death and Burial in the Roman World*. Baltimore: The John Hopkins University Press, 1971.

Trump, Donald J. and Bill Zanker. *Think Big*. New York: Harper, 2007.

Trump, Donald J. and Tony Schwartz. *Trump: The Art of the Deal*. New York: Ballantine Books, 1987.

Tucker, Joan Romanosky. *From Field to Table: Visual Images of Food in the Western Roman Empire*. Master's thesis, University of Georgia, 2002.

Twede, Diana. "Commercial Amphoras: The Earliest Consumer Packages?" *Journal of Macromarketing* 22, no. 1, (2002): 98–108.

Verhoef, Peter C. and Katherine N. Lemon.
"Successful Customer Value Management:
Key Lessons and Emerging Trends."
European Management Journal no. 31,
(2013): 1–15.

Will, E. L. "The Ancient Commercial Amphora."
Archaeology no. 30, (1977): 264–278.

Zanker, Paul. *The Power of Images in the Age of
Augustus*. Ann Arbor: The University of
Michigan Press, 1990.

Endnotes

Introduction

[1] Thomas C. Mann and Janet Greene, *Over Their Dead Bodies: Yankee Epitaphs & History* (Brattleboro: The Stephen Greene Press, 1962), 37.

[2] There are many other models of the consumer buying process. See Philip Kotler, Kevin Lane Keller, and Peggy H. Cunningham, *Marketing Management,* Canadian 12th ed. (Toronto: Pearson Prentice Hall, 2006), 209–211.

[3] The three-stage customer acquisition process that is the focus of this text is a variation of the more traditional multistep customer development process (Kotler et al., *Marketing Management,* 165). The four key related steps are Suspects → Prospects → First Time Customers → Repeat Customers.

[4] Kotler et al., *Marketing Management*, 200.

[5] Ibid.

[6] Ibid., 200–209.

[7] Ibid., 201.

[8] Peter C. Verhoef and Katherine N. Lemon, "Successful Customer Value Management: Key Lessons and Emerging Trends," *European Management Journal* no. 31, (2013): 8.

[9] Robert I. Curtis, "A Personalized Floor Mosaic from Pompeii," *American Journal of Archeology*, 88, no. 4, (1984): 563–4.

[10] Caesar claimed he was descended from the goddess Venus.

[11] This image (or other media file) is in the public domain. From: http://en.wikipedia. org/wiki/File:CiceroBust.jpg (accessed September 20, 2012).

[12] Cicero, *In Catilinam,* vol. 4 (Cambridge: Harvard University Press, 1977),17. All quotations of Cicero's *In Catilinam* , unless noted otherwise, are taken from MacDonald.

[13] Cicero, *On Duties* (Cambridge: Harvard University Press, 2005), 150. All quotations of Cicero's *On Duties*, unless noted otherwise, are taken from Miller.

[14] Suetonius, *Augustus and Nero,* vol. 4. (Cambridge: Harvard University Press, 2001), 2. *Augustus* IV. 2. All translations of

Suetonius, unless noted otherwise, are taken from Rolfe.

[15] This image (or other media file) is in the public domain. From: https://en.wikipedia.org/wiki/File:Augustus (accessed June 4, 2013).

[16] David Jones, *The Bankers of Puteoli: Finance, Trade and Industry in the Roman World* (Gloucestershire: Tempus Publishing Limited, 2006), 172. Note: Equestrians were aristocrats, but inferior to senators.

[17] Pliny the Elder, *Natural History,* vol. 9 (Cambridge: Harvard University Press, 2005), 67. Pliny wrote "people who in their complaints about luxury used to protest that cooks were being bought at a higher price per man than a horse; but now the price for three horses is given for a cook . . . ." All quotations of Pliny the Elder, Vols. 8–11, unless noted otherwise, are taken from Rackham.

[18] Sandra Joshel, *Work, Identity, and Legal Status at Rome: A Study of Occupational Inscriptions* (Norman: University of Oklahoma Press, 1992), 55.

[19] Ibid.

[20] Lawrence Keppie, *Understanding Roman Inscriptions* (Baltimore: The John Hopkins University Press, 1991), 101.

[21] Joshel, *Work, Identity, and Legal Status at Rome,* 112.

[22] Maureen Carroll, *Spirits of the Dead: Roman Funerary Commemoration in Western Europe* (Oxford: Oxford University Press, 2006), 55.

[23] Penelope J. E. Davies, *Death and the Emperor* (Austin: University of Texas Press, 2004),121.

[24] Peter J. Holliday, ed., *Narrative and Event in Ancient Art* (Cambridge: Cambridge University Press, 1993), 317.

[25] Plutarch, *The Parallel Lives*, "The Life of Brutus," 5.

[26] Brian K. Harvey, *Roman Lives, Ancient Roman Lives as Illustrated by Latin Inscriptions* (Newburyport: Focus Publishing, 2004), CIL 6.1635, 28.

[27] Joshel, *Work, Identity, and Legal Status at Rome*, 60.

[28] Harvey, CIL 6.9980, 88. Identified as a second century AD inscription because Cocceia Phyllis was possibly a freedwoman of the Emperor Nerva.

[29] Harvey, CIL 6.7655, 172. Inscription date unknown.

[30] Harvey, CIL 6.9822, 175. Identified as a first century AD inscription.

[31] Harvey, CIL 6.9221, 174. Inscription date unknown. The Via Sacra was a main street through the Forum in ancient Rome.

[32] Image from *Corpus Inscriptionum Latinarum*, VI 9221cf. VI, 3895.

[33] The title of Kenneth Roman's 2009 biography of Ogilvy.

[34] David Ogilvy died in 1999 at 88.

[35] Constance L. Hays, "David Ogilvy, 88, Father of Soft Sell In Advertising, Dies," *New York Times*, July 22, 1999. Accessed 9/22/12. http://www.nytimes.com/1999/07/22/business/david-ogilvy-88-father-of-soft-sell-in-advertising-dies.html?pagewanted=all&src=pm

[36] Kenneth Roman, *The King of Madison Avenue: David Ogilvy and the Making of Modern Advertising* (New York: PalgraveMacMillan, 2009), 116.

[37] Ibid., 4.

[38] Glen Plaskin, "Playboy Interview: Donald Trump," *Playboy* 37, no. 3, (1990), 55.

[39] Donald J. Trump and Tony Schwartz, *Trump: The Art of the Deal* (New York: Ballantine Books, 1987), 1.

[40] Donald J. Trump and Bill Zanker, *Think Big* (New York: Harper, 2007), 41.

[41] This image (or other media file) is in the public domain. From: http://en.wikipedia.org/wiki/File:Donald_Trump (accessed June 4, 2013).

[42] John Markoff, "Steven P. Jobs, 1955–2011 Apple's Visionary Redefined Digital Age," *New York Times*, October 5, 2011. Accessed October 26, 2013. http://www.nytimes.com/2011/10/06/business/steve-jobs-of-apple-dies-at-56.html?pagewanted=all&_r=0

[43] Kristen Schweizer, "Apple Overtakes Coca-Cola as World's Most Valuable Brand," *Bloomberg*, September 30, 2013. Accessed October 26, 2013. http://www.bloomberg.com/news/2013-09-30/apple-overtakes-coca-cola-as-most-valuable-brand-study-finds.html

Chapter 1

[1] Juvenal, *Satires*, 10, translated by Susanna Morton Braund (Cambridge: Harvard University Press, 2004), 77–80. All quotations of Juvenal, unless noted otherwise, are taken from Braund.

[2] Paul Erdkamp, *The Grain Market in the Roman Empire: A social, political and economic study* (Cambridge: Cambridge University Press, 2005), 241–242.

[3] Suetonius, *Augustus* XLII,3.

[4] Erdkamp, *The Grain Market in the Roman Empire*, 240–241.

[5] Lauren Hackworth Petersen, "The Baker, His Tomb, His Wife, and Her Breadbasket: The Monument of Eurysaces in Rome," *The Art Bulletin* 85, no. 2, (2003): 117.

College Art Association. Accessed January 4, 2010. *AccessMyLibrary.* http//www. accessmylibrary.com Petersen cites the following Republican periods as having acute grain shortages and riots in Rome: 58–56 BC, 43–36 BC, and 30s–20s BC.

[6] Barbara Levick, *Claudius,* (New Haven: Yale University Press, 1990), 109.

[7] This image (or other media file) is in the public domain. From:http://en.wikipedia.org/ wiki/File:Claudius (accessed June 4, 2013).

[8] James G. Crossley, *The Date of Mark's Gospel* (London: Bloomsbury T&T Clark International, 2004), 1.

[9] Mark 8:4. All biblical quotations, unless noted otherwise, are taken from *The New American Bible* (1981).

[10] This image (or other media file) is in the public domain. From:http://upload.wikimedia.org/ wikipedia/commons/6/67/Christ_feeding_ the_multitude.jpg (accessed September 20, 2012).

[11] Mark 6:37.

[12] Erdkamp, *The Grain Market in the Roman Empire,* 253.

[13] This image (or other media file) is in the public domain. From: http://en.wikipedia. org/wiki/File:Pompei_-_House_of_Julia_ Felix_-_2_-_MAN.jpg (accessed September 20, 2012).

[14] Eurysaces' status as a freedman is still debated by historians, but that debate is irrelevant to our discussion here. See Petersen (2011).

[15] Lauren Hackworth Petersen, *The Freedman in Roman Art and Art History* (Cambridge: Cambridge University Press, 2011), 90. Petersen estimates the construction of Eurysaces' tomb as between the middle and late first century BC.

[16] As judged by the size of his surviving tomb.

[17] "History of Sandwich Kent: Origin of the Sandwich," *Open* Sandwich, accessed September 19, 2012, http://www.open-sandwich.co.uk/town_history/sandwich_origin.htm

[18] Lauren Hackworth Petersen, *The Art Bulletin* 85, no. 2, (2003):87. College Art Association. Accessed January 4, 2010. *AccessMyLibrary.* http//www.accessmylibrary.com

[19] Petersen, *The Freedman in Roman Art and Art History*, 87–88.

[20] Petersen, "The Baker, His Tomb, His Wife, and Her Breadbasket," 10.

[21] Paul Zanker, *The Power of Images in the Age of Augustus,* (Ann Arbor: The University of Michigan Press, 1990), 291.

[22] Keppie, *Understanding Roman Inscriptions*, 100–101.

[23] David Ogilvy, *Ogilvy on Advertising* (New York: Vintage Books, 1985), 11–12.

[24] Bob Garfield, "Ad Age Advertising Century: The Top 100 Campaigns," *Advertising* Age, accessed October 18, 2012, http://adage.com/article/special-report-the-advertising-century/ad-age-advertising-century-top-100-campaigns/140918/

[25] Dominik Imseng, *Think Small: The Story of the World's Greatest Ad* (Full Stop Press, 2011), 78.

[26] Ibid., 103.

[27] Thomas E. Bonsall, *Disaster in Dearborn: The Story of the Edsel* (Stanford: Stanford University Press, 2002), 109–117.

[28] Ibid., 126.

[29] Bo Burlingham and George Gendron, "The Entrepreneur of the Decade," *Inc. Magazine*, April 1989, http://www.inc.com/magazine/19890401/5602.html (accessed June 10, 2014).

[30] David Ogilvy, *Confessions of an Advertising Man*, (Harpenden: Southbank Publishing, 2011), 116.

[31] Petersen, *The Freedman in Roman Art and Art History*, 99.

[32] Ogilvy, *Confessions of an Advertising Man*, 113.

[33] See chapter fifteen of Walter Isaacson's biography, *Steve Jobs.*

[34] Petersen, *The Freedman in Roman Art and Art History,* 88.

[35] This image (or other media file) is in the public domain. From: http://en.wikipedia.org/wiki/File:Piranesi-3052.jpg (accessed June 18, 2013).

[36] J. M. C. Toynbee, *Death and Burial in the Roman World* (Baltimore: The John Hopkins University Press, 1971), 128.

[37] Agnes Crawford, "Eclectic Exoticism and Funerary Bling: The Pyramid of Gaius Cestius," *Understanding Rome* (blog), http://understandingrome.wordpress.com/2013/02/05/eclectic- exoticism-and-funerary bling-the-pyramid-of-gaius-cestius/

[38] Keppie, *Understanding Roman Inscriptions,* 104–105.

[39] Access granted courtesy of the Ministry of Cultural Heritage and Activities.

[40] Ian A. Richmond, *The City Wall of Imperial Rome* (Yardley: Westholme Publishing, 2013) 207.

[41] Petersen, "The Baker, His Tomb, His Wife, and Her Breadbasket," 17.

[42] Ibid., 110.

[43] Olle Brandt, "Recent Research on the Tomb of Eurysaces," *Opuscula Romana* 19, no. 2, (1993): 15.

[44] Petersen, "The Baker, His Tomb, His Wife, and Her Breadbasket," 14.

[45] Travertine, a form of limestone, was used by the Roman elite on tombs, temples, baths and even the Colosseum. From: http://en.wikipedia.org/wiki/Travertine (accessed June 19, 2013).

[46] Petersen, "The Baker, His Tomb, His Wife, and Her Breadbasket," 14.

[47] Ibid.

[48] Ogilvy, *Ogilvy on Advertising*, 94–95.

[49] Paul Messaris, *Visual Persuasion: The Role of Images in Advertising* (Thousand Oaks: SAGE Publications, Inc, 1997) 19–20. Here, Messaris discussed the alteration and use of the *Mona Lisa* in an advertisement for Prince Spaghetti.

[50] Ibid., 59–62. Messaris also reports that sharp-angled shapes (for example, triangles and stars) are found to be more distinctive than round or right-angled shapes. Thus, the nonsymmetrical trapezoid of Eurysaces would likely have been even more impactful to the viewer than traditional round or square tombs.

Chapter 2

[1] Petersen, "The Baker, His Tomb, His Wife, and Her Breadbasket," 20, note 2.

[2] Ibid., 17.

[3] Ogilvy, *Confessions of an Advertising Man,* 115.

[4] Ibid., 117.

[5] Judie Lannon, "Asking the Right Questions: What Do People Do with Advertising?" in *Brand Equity & Advertising,* edited by David A. Aaker and Alexander L. Biel (Hillsdale: Lawrence Erlbaum Associates, 1993), 170.

[6] Petersen, "The Baker, His Tomb, His Wife, and Her Breadbasket," 4. The inscription does not include an *L* or *Lib,* both abbreviations for *Libertinus,* a freed male slave.

[7] Petersen, *The Freedman in Roman Art and Art History,* 87. On page 98, the author also points out that the absence of any information about Eurysaces' father in the inscription indicates a servile past.

[8] Ibid.

[9] Ibid., 117. According to Petersen, shortages occurred often during the Republic's collapse.

[10] Professor Carlon, in discussions with the author, indicated that the listing might alternatively be chronological (latest to earliest), as was typical of the Roman elite.

[11] Petersen, *Petersen The Freedman in Roman Art and Art History, 106.*

[12] Ibid.

[13] Petersen, "The Baker, His Tomb, His Wife, and Her Breadbasket," 12.

[14] Ibid., 11.

[15] Joan Romanosky Tucker, *From Field to Table: Visual Images of Food in the Western Roman Empire,* Master's thesis, University of Georgia, 2002, 61, fig. 58. It is also feasible that one or more of the togate officials represent Eurysaces (Petersen *The Freedman in Roman Art and Art History,* 106).

[16] Ibid.

[17] Ogilvy, *Ogilvy on Advertising,* 80.

[18] Roman, *The King of Madison Avenue,* 61.

[19] Ogilvy, *Confessions of an Advertising Man,* 113. Ogilvy writing in 1963, specifically said, "The consumer isn't a moron; she is your wife."

[20] Erdkamp, *The Grain Market in the Roman Empire,* 252, argues that the state's "most direct way to intervene in the grain and bread supply of the Roman populace was to control the activities of the bakers." Erdkamp also indicates that "authorities systematically sold public

> grain to merchants, who in turn sold it to consumers in Rome."

[21] Ogilvy, *Ogilvy on Advertising*, 107.

[22] See, for example, Petronius, *The Satyricon*, 71.

[23] Anne Marie Kelly, "Scented Ads: Not Just for Perfume Anymore,"*Forbes.com*, January 17, 2012. http://www.forbes.com/sites/annemariekelly/2012/01/17/scented-ads-not-just-for-perfume-anymore/ (accessed June 26, 2014).

[24] Jameson Fink, "Scratch-and-Sniff Wine Label," *Foodista*, June 27, 2011. http://www.foodista.com/blog/2011/06/27/scratch-and-sniff-wine-label (accessed June 26, 2014).

[25] Petersen, "The Baker, His Tomb, His Wife, and Her Breadbasket," 3.

[26] Petersen, *The Freedman in Roman Art and Art History*, 93–95. Petersen also suggests that it is possible that the portraits of Eurysaces and Atista, as well as the epitaph could have belonged to a nearby tomb of another baker named Ogulnius.

[27] Ogilvy, *Ogilvy on Advertising*, 103.

[28] Ogilvy, *Confessions of an Advertising Man*, 114.

[29] Keppie, *Understanding Roman Inscriptions*, 100.

[30] Vitruvius, *On Architecture*, 1.10. All translations of Vitruvius, unless noted otherwise, are from Granger.

[31] Petersen, *The Freedman in Roman Art and Art History*, 257, note 61.

[32] Penelope J. E. Davies, *Death and the Emperor* (Austin: University of Texas Press, 2004), 13.

[33] Ibid., 14.

[34] Ibid., 13.

[35] Petronius, *The Satyricon*, 71. All translations of Petronius, unless noted otherwise, are taken from Arrowsmith.

[36] Ogilvy, *Confessions of an Advertising Man*, 116.

[37] Ibid., 154.

[38] Petersen, *The Freedman in Roman Art and Art History*, 109.

[39] This work is in the in the public domain. From:http://commons.wikimedia.org/wiki/File:001_Conrad_Cichorius,_Die_Reliefs_der_Traianssäule,_Tafel_I.jpg (accessed June 20, 2013).

[40] Wikipedia contributors, "Trajan's Column," *Wikipedia, The Free Encyclopedia*, http://en.wikipedia.org/wiki/Trajan's_Column

Chapter 3

[1] N. S. Gill, "Toga,"*AboutEducation,* http://
    ancienthistory.about.com/od/clothing/
    a/063010-Toga.htm (accessed October 25,
    2013).

[2] Found on the Ara Pacis in Rome.

[3] Vergil, *Aeneid,* 1.282. All translations of Virgil,
    unless noted otherwise, are taken from
    McCrorie.

[4] Suetonius, *Augustus* (LXXIII.1). All translations
    of Suetonius, unless noted otherwise, are
    taken from Rolfe.

[5] A. H. M. Jones, "The Cloth Industry under the Roman
    Empire." *The Economic History Review,*
    Second Series 13, no. 2, (1960), 184.

[6] Ibid.

[7] Ibid., 190.

[8] Ibid.

[9] Walter Moeller, *The Wool Trade of Ancient Pompeii:
    Studies of the Dutch Archeological &
    Historical Society* (Leiden: E. J. Brill,
    1976), 35–51; R. P. Duncan-Jones,
    "Review of the Wool Trade of Ancient
    Pompeii by Walter O. Moeller," *The
    Classical Review,* New Series 29, no. 1
    (1979):190–191.

[10] Moeller, *The Wool Trade of Ancient Pompeii,* 31–56.

[11] Mary R. Lefkowitz and Maureen B. Fant, "Women's Life in Greece and Rome," *Stoa.org,* http://www.stoa.org/diotima/ anthology/wlgr/wlgr-publiclife196.shtml (accessed October 27, 2013).

[12] John H. Stambaugh, *The Ancient Roman City* (Baltimore: John Hopkins University Press, 1998), 264.

[13] Ibid.

[14] Joseph H. Frankl, "Whose Forum? Imperial and Elite Patronage in the Forum of Pompeii," *Studies in Mediterranean Antiquity and Classics* 3, no. 1, Article 3, (2013): 4.

[15] Moeller, *The Wool Trade of Ancient Pompeii,* 57.

[16] August Mau, *Pompeii: Its Life and Art,* translated by Francis Willey Kelsey (New York: The Macmillan Company, 1899), 110.

[17] This image (or other media file) in the public domain. From: http://www.gutenberg. org/files/42715/42715-h/42715-h. htm#Page_110 (accessed October 22, 2013).

[18] Moeller, *The Wool Trade of Ancient Pompeii,* 56.

[19] Mau, *Pompeii: Its Life and Art,* 110.

[20] Moeller, *The Wool Trade of Ancient Pompeii,* 61.

[21] This image (or other media file) in the public domain. From: http://www.gutenberg. org/files/42715/42715-h/42715-h. htm#Page_116 (accessed October 22, 2013).

[22] Paul Zanker in his book *The Power of Images in the Age of Augustus* suggests that the marble work on Eumachia's building came from Rome, possibly from the same workshop that produced the Ara Pacis for the Emperor Augustus; 320; 322, fig. 252 a; 323, fig. b).

[23] Mau, *Pompeii: Its Life and Art*, 111.

[24] Frankl, "Whose Forum?" 9.

[25] Trump and Zanker, *Think Big*, 274.

[26] Ibid., 285.

[27] Walter Isaacson, *Steve Jobs,* (New York: Simon & Schuster, 2011), 162.

[28] Ibid., 165.

[29] Mau, *Pompeii: Its Life and Art*, 112.

[30] This image (or other media file) is in the public domain. From: http://www.gutenberg.org/ files/42715/42715-h/42715-h.htm#fig255

[31] Mau, *Pompeii: Its Life and Art*, 385.

[32] Ibid.

[33] Moeller, *The Wool Trade of Ancient Pompeii*, 75.

[34] This image (or other media file) in the public domain. From: http://www.gutenberg.org/files/42715/42715-h/42715-h.htm#fig225

[35] Moeller, *The Wool Trade of Ancient Pompeii*, 20, 96.

[36] Suetonius, *Vespasian* (23.3).

[37] Walter Moeller, "The Building of Eumachia: A Reconsideration," *American Journal of Archeology* 76, no.3 (1972):323–327.

[38] Verhoef and Lemon, "*Successful Customer Value Management*," 10.

[39] Shelton, *As the Romans Did*, (New York: Oxford University Press, 1998), 19.

[40] Ibid., 52–53.

[41] Professor Carlon, in discussions with the author, pointed out that Eumachia was not unique as a patron. There is evidence for women as patrons in other Italian towns; see Forbis (1990).

[42] Elaine Fantham, Helen Peet Foley, Natalie Boyem Kampen, Sarah B. Pomeroy, and H. Alan Shapiro, *Women in the Classical World,* (New York: Oxford University Press, 1994), 340.

[43] The campaign was also a not so subtle shot at IBM, a competitor of Apple that trademarked and still uses the slogan "THINK." *Mad Magazine* even satirized the slogan as THIMK. For more on THINK, see http://www-03.ibm.com/ibm/

history/exhibits/attic2/attic2_207.html
and http://www-03.ibm.com/ibm/history/
ibm100/us/en/forum/

[44] From: http://en.wikipedia.org/wiki/File:Apple_
logo_Think_Different_vectorized.svg.
(accessed: October 22, 2013).

[45] Isaacson, *Steve Jobs,* 330.

[46] Ibid., 329.

[47] Ray Laurence, *Roman Pompeii* (London: Rutledge,
1994), 28, lists the building as public in
his text, whereas Michael Scott, *Space and
Society in the Greek and Roman Worlds*
(Cambridge: Cambridge University Press,
2012) refers to the building as one of the
city's largest private structures.

[48] Mau, *Pompeii: Its Life and Art,* 110.

[49] Professor Carlon, in discussions with the author,
indicated that Eumachia's inscription
might refer to an existing structure's
embellishment.

[50] "Global Ad Spend Grows 3.2% in 2012," *Nielsen,*
April 11, 2013, http://nielsen.com/us/en/
newswire/2013/global-ad-spend-grows-3.2-
percent-in-2012.html (accessed October
24, 2013).

[51] Louise Story, "Home Equity Frenzy Was a
Bank Ad Come True," *The New York
Times,* August 14, 2008, http://www.
nytimes.com/2008/08/15/business/15sell.

html?pagewanted=all&_r=0 (accessed October 24, 2013).

[52] This is a prepared text of the commencement address to the graduating students of Stanford University delivered by Steve Jobs, CEO of Apple Computer and of Pixar Animation Studios, on June 12, 2005, http://news.stanford.edu/news/2005/june15/jobs-061505.html (accessed October 25, 2013).

Chapter 4

[1] Robert I. Curtis, "A Personalized Floor Mosaic from Pompeii," *American Journal of Archeology*, 88, no. 4, (1984):563–564.

[2] Pliny, *Natural History*, 31.93. All quotations of Pliny the Elder, Bks. 28–32, unless noted otherwise, are taken from Jones.

[3] From: http://en.wikisource.org/wiki/Moral_letters_to_Lucilius/Letter_95.25 (accessed June 20, 2013).

[4] Martial, *Epigrams*, 11.27.1. All translations of Martial, unless noted otherwise, are taken from Shackleton Bailey.

[5] Ibid., 6.93.5.

[6] Ibid., 13.82.

[7] Pliny *Natural History* 31.97–98.

[8] Ibid., 31.94.

[9] Ibid.

[10] Robert I. Curtis, "Umami and the Foods of Classical Antiquity," *American Journal of Clinical Nutrition,* doi: 10.3945/ajcn.2009.27462C 90, no. 3, (2009):713s.

[11] Ibid., 716s.

[12] From: https://en.wikipedia.org/wiki/File:Garumamphoren.JPG (accessed June 20, 2013).

[13] Curtis, *"Umami and the Foods of Classical Antiquity,"* 713s.

[14] Robert I. Curtis, "Product Identification and Advertising on Roman Commercial Amphorae," *Ancient Society* 15–17, (1984–6):.211.

[15] Ibid., 217.

[16] Ibid., 217; 218–19 further strengthens his argument that these words constitute advertising by also discussing inferior versions (seconds) of fish-sauce that carry the word SEC (undum) as well as other less frequently used descriptors.

[17] Ibid., 221–223.

[18] Ibid., 225.

[19] Ibid., 226.

[20] Pliny, *Natural History,* 31.94.

[21] Ogilvy, *Confessions of an Advertising Man*,152.

[22] Ogilvy, *Ogilvy on Advertising*, 111.

[23] Curtis, "Product Identification and Advertising on Roman Commercial Amphorae," 216.

[24] From: http://terroirs.denfrance.free.fr/p/ encyclopedie/garum.html (accessed June 27, 2014).

[25] Curtis, *"Umami and the Foods of Classical Antiquity,"* 716s.

[26] Curtis, "Product Identification and Advertising on Roman Commercial Amphorae," 225.

[27] Scaurus' dominant market position has also earned him the modern title of "The Ketchup King" because before the early nineteenth century, ketchup was tomato-free, and it might be a descendant of garum; see Andrew F. Smith, *Pure Ketchup: A History of America's National Condiment* (Columbia: University of South Carolina Press, 1996), 7.

[28] Curtis, "Product Identification and Advertising on Roman Commercial Amphorae," 225..

[29] Ibid., 227–8.

[30] Stewart Owen, "The Lando ImagePower Survey: A Global Assessment of Brand Strength," in *Brand Equity & Advertising*, edited by Aaker, David A. and Alexander L. Biel (Hillsdale: Lawrence Erlbaum Associates,

1993), 16. Continuity, longevity, and quality have been shown to strongly influence a brand's success.

[31] Curtis, "*Umami and the Foods of Classical Antiquity*," 716s.

[32] Curtis, "*A Personalized Floor Mosaic from Pompeii*," 559–61).

[33] Ibid., 563.

[34] Curtis, "*Umami and the Foods of Classical Antiquity*," 716s.

[35] From: https://en.wikipedia.org/wiki/File:Garum_Mosaik_Pompeji.JPG (accessed June 21, 2013).

[36] "Dictionary," *American Marketing Association*, http://www.marketingpower.com/_layouts/Dictionary.aspx?dLetter=B (accessed June 21, 2013).

[37] Ogilvy, *Confessions of an Advertising Man*, 152.

[38] Ibid., 117.

[39] Karl Moore and Susan Reid, "The Birth of Brand: 4000 years of Branding," *Business History* 50, no. 4, (2008): 429.

[40] Ibid., 429–430).

[41] Kotler et al., *Marketing Management*, 276.

[42] Ibid., 277.

[43] Alexander L. Biel, "Converting Image into Equity," in *Brand Equity* & *Advertis*ing, edited by

Aaker, David A. and Alexander L. Biel (Hillsdale: Lawrence Erlbaum Associates, Publishers, 1993), 69.

[44] Piotr (Rzeszow)Berdowski, "Roman Businesswomen,1: The case of the producers and distributors of garum in Pompeii." *Analecta Archaeologica Ressoviensia*, (2008): 251–269.

[45] Roman, *The King of Madison Avenue*, 6. "It didn't occur to Ogilvy that race or religion should be an issue in hiring the best people."

[46] Ogilvy, *Ogilvy on Advertising*, 46.

Chapter 5

[1] Herbert Hoover, address at Des Moines, Iowa, October 4, 1932, *The Public Papers of the Presidents of the United States: Herbert Hoover*, 1932–1933, 467. http://en.wikiquote.org/wiki/Herbert_Hoover (accessed May 17, 2013).

[2] This image is in the public domain. Bust of Cicero was done by Bertel Thorvaldsen in 1799–1800. Photo by Gunnar Bach Pedersen. From: http://commons.wikimedia.org/wiki/Marcus_Tullius_Cicero#mediaviewer/File:Thorvaldsen_Cicero.jpg (accessed June 28, 2014).

[3] Cicero, *Letters to Atticus*, 97.3; Robert Lerner, *Career Turbulence: Ancient Lessons for Survival*

in the Modern Workplace (Oshawa: Multi-Media Publications, 2014), 100–101.

[4] The image of Marcus Brutus is in the public domain. From:https://upload.wikimedia.org/wikipedia/commons/e/e9/Portrait_Brutus_Massimo.jpg (Accessed June 27, 2013).

[5] Rex Stem, *The Political Biographies of Cornelius Nepos* (Ann Arbor: The University of Michigan Press, 2012), 15.

[6] Ibid.

[7] Cicero, *Letters to Atticus*, Vol.1, 17. All translations of Cicero's *Letters to Atticus*, unless noted otherwise, are taken from Shackleton Bailey.

[8] This image is in the public domain. From: http://en.wikipedia.org/wiki/File:Svedomsky-Fulvia (accessed June 23, 2013).

[9] Stem, *The Political Biographies of Cornelius Nepos,* 59.

[10] Nepos, *Cato*, 3.5. All translations of Nepos, unless noted otherwise, are taken from Rolfe.

[11] Nepos, *Atticus*, 13.7.

[12] Trump and Zanker, *Think Big,* 150.

[13] Nicholas Horsfall, "Prose and Mime," *Latin Literature*, edited by E. J. Kenney and W. V. Clausen (Cambridge University Press, 1982), *Cambridge Histories Online*, 290–293.

[14] Stem, *The Political Biographies of Cornelius Nepos,* vii.

[15] Trump and Zanker, *Think Big,* 154.

[16] H. Hill, *The Roman Middle Class in the Republican Period* (Westport: Greenwood Press, 1974), 83. "The main reason why provincial communities or individuals contracted debt was, no doubt, in order to pay their tribute" to Rome.

[17] Nepos, *Atticus*, II.4.

[18] Trump and Zanker, *Think Big,* 87.

[19] Nepos, *Atticus*, II.6.

[20] Cicero, *Letters to Atticus*, 121.1.

[21] Ibid.

[22] Nepos *Atticus* III.2.

[23] Ryan Messmore, "Charitable Giving Benefits Giver as Much as Receiver,"*Foxnews. com*, December 22, 2006, http://www. foxnews.com/story/2006/12/22/charitable-giving-benefits-giver-as-much-as-receiver/ (accessed July 11, 2014).

[24] Trump and Zanker, *Think Big,* 219.

[25] Nepos, *Atticus*, XV.1.

[26] Nepos, *Atticus ,*VI.5.

[27] Nepos, *Atticus*, XIII.5.

[28] Nepos, *Atticus*, III.1.

Chapter 6

[1] Cicero, *Letters to Atticus*, 83.2.

[2] Cicero, *Letters to Atticus*, 82.4.

[3] Cicero, *Letters to Atticus*, 13.1, 19.9, 20.4, 21.10, 33.2, and 41.6.

[4] Cicero, *Letters to Atticus*, 13.1.

[5] Pliny, *Natural History*, 35.127. All quotations of Pliny the Elder, Bks. 33-–35, unless noted otherwise, are taken from Rackham.

[6] Alice Hill Byrne, *Titus Pomponius Atticus: Chapters of a Biography* (Lexington: Bibliolife, LLC, 2009), 39.

[7] This image is in the public domain. From: https://en.wikipedia.org/wiki/File:Cesar-sa_mort.jpg (accessed June 24, 2013).

[8] This image is in the public domain. From: https://en.wikipedia.org/wiki/File:Eid_Mar.jpg (accessed June 24, 2013).

[9] Attributed to Winston Churchill.

[10] Curtis, "Umami and the Foods of Classical Antiquity," 715s.

[11] Curtis, "A Personalized Floor Mosaic from Pompeii," 563.

[12] Ibid., 566.

[13] Cicero, *On Duties*, 1.150.

[14] Curtis, "A Personalized Floor Mosaic from Pompeii," 562.

[15] Mau, *Pompeii: Its Life and Art*, 411.

[16] Plaskin, "Playboy Interview: Donald Trump."

[17] Attributed to Spike Milligan. From: http:// www.brainyquote.com/quotes/quotes/s/ spikemilli392234.html (accessed September 13, 2013).

[18] Michael Scott, *Space and Society in the Greek and Roman Worlds* (Cambridge: Cambridge University Press, 2012), 91.

[19] Ibid.

[20] Ibid.

[21] Alison E. Cooley and M. G. L. Cooley, *Pompeii and Herculaneum: A Sourcebook* (London: Routledge, 2014), 145.

[22] Mau, *Pompeii: Its Life and Art*, 216.

[23] Scott, *Space and Society in the Greek and Roman Worlds*, 88; Cooleys, *Pompeii and Herculaneum*, 144.

[24] Cooleys, *Pompeii and Herculaneum*, 145.

[25] Apuleius, *The Golden Ass*, translated by William Adlington (Hertfordshire: Wadsworth Editions Limited, 1996).

[26] Adlington, *The Golden Ass*, ix.

[27] Apuleius, *The Golden Ass*, 143–4. All translations of Apuleius, unless noted otherwise, are from Adlington as revised by Gaselee.

[28] Ibid., 144.

[29] George Galavarius, *Bread and the Liturgy: The Symbolism of the Early Christian and Byzantine Bread Stamps* (Madison: The University of Wisconsin Press, 1970), 26.

[30] John Bodel, *Roman Brick Stamps in the Kelsey Museum* (Ann Arbor: The University of Michigan Press, 1983), 1. ". . . Latin inscriptions that first appear on Roman bricks during the last century of the Republic."

[31] Pliny, *Natural History*, 33.26.

[32] Mau, *Pompeii: Its Life and Art*, 498. Actual impression in Latin reads *(C)elerius Q. Grani Verr ser.*

[33] This image is in the public domain. From: http://en.wikipedia.org/wiki/File:Roda_de_Vitruvi.jpg (accessed June 24, 2013).

[34] Serajul Quadir and Ruma Paul, "Bangladesh factory fire kills 8; collapse toll tops 900," *Reuters*, May 9, 2013, http://www.reuters.com/article/2013/05/09/us-bangladesh-fire-idUSBRE94801T20130509 (accessed June 2, 2013).

[35] Jasmin Malik Chua, "Garment-Factory Fire in Pakistan Kills 300 Trapped Behind Locked Doors," by Jasmin Malik Chua, September 13, 2012, *http://www.ecouterre.com/garment-factory-fire-in-pakistan-kills-300-trapped-behind-locked-doors/* (accessed June 2, 2013).

[36] Gordon Brown, "India Must Ban Child Labor," *Huffington Post*, December 12, 2012, http://www.huffingtonpost.com/gordon-

brown/india-child-labor-laws_b_2345756. html (accessed June 2, 2013).

[37] See Vance Packard's 1957 classic, *The Hidden Persuaders.*

Appendix A

[1] Petronius, *The Satyricon*, 77–78.

[2] Andrej Petrovic, "Under Full Sail: Trimalchio's Way to Eternity. A Note on Petr. Sat. 7.19–7.10," *Acta Ant. Hung* 45, (2005): 89. *Academia.edu,* http://www. academia.edu/942701/Under_Full_Sail_ Trimalchios_Way_into_Eternity._A_ Note_on_Petr._Sat._71.9–10 (accessed September 19, 2013).

[3] Ibid., 87.

[4] Suetonius, *Nero*, LII.1.

[5] Professor Carlon, in discussions with the author, indicated that Petronius' sharp wit might also have been aimed at Seneca in this instance.

Appendix B

[1] Ilaria Gozzini Giacose, *A Taste of Ancient Rome* (Chicago: The University of Chicago Press, 1994), 29.

Customer Aquisition Strategies

Index of Ancient Names

Customer Aquisition Strategies

About The Author

B ob is a retired business executive whose career spanned more than 30 years in the high tech industry. Bob began his professional career at Xerox Corporation after he obtained a Bachelor of Science degree in Physics from Worcester Polytechnic Institute and an MBA from the University of Rochester's Simon School of Business.

In 1980 Bob joined Wang Laboratories and spent twenty years with Wang and its successor companies in a variety of product development, marketing, sales and service management positions. Following Wang's emergence from bankruptcy in 1993 as Wang Global, Bob was named President of Wang Canada and following his turnaround of that operation, Bob was appointed President of Wang Global's North American Field Service operation with responsibility for over 4,000 employees and revenues of more than half a billion dollars.

In 2000, following Getronics NV's acquisition of Wang Global, Bob led a management buyout of a division of Getronics and was appointed President and CEO of QualxServ, the newly formed company. Under Bob's leadership QualxServ grew into a global computer services provider spanning more than a dozen countries and employing over 3,000 computer service professionals worldwide.

After spending nearly a decade with QualxServ, Bob retired from his position as President and CEO in 2009 and stepped down from QualxServ's Board in 2010 (the company has since been renamed Worldwide TechServices). Retirement has allowed Bob to spend more time with his wife Diane and daughters Meredith and Allison as well as pursue his passion for the study of the business management lessons that can be learned from ancient Rome.

In addition to this text Bob is the author of *Entrepreneurship and Ethics in Ancient Rome, The Management Lessons of Pliny the Younger* and *Career Turbulence, Ancient Lessons for Survival in the Modern Workplace*. Bob also remains a consultant to Worldwide TechServices, serves as an advisor to Work Market and is a member of the George Eastman Circle at the University of Rochester.

About the Series

This series is for primarily business and IT professionals looking for inspiration for their projects. Specifically, business managers responsible for solving business problems, or Project Managers (PMs) responsible for delivering business solutions through IT projects.

This series uses relevant historical case studies to examine how historical projects and emerging technologies of the past solved complex problems. It then draws comparisons to challenges encountered in today's IT projects.

This series benefits the reader in several ways:

- It outlines the stages involved in delivering a complex IT project providing a step-by-step guide to the project deliverables.

- It vividly describes the crucial lessons from historical projects and complements these with some of today's best practices.

- It makes the whole learning experience more memorable.

The series should inspire the reader as these historical projects were achieved with a lesser (inferior) technology.

Website: **http://www.lessons-from-history.com/**

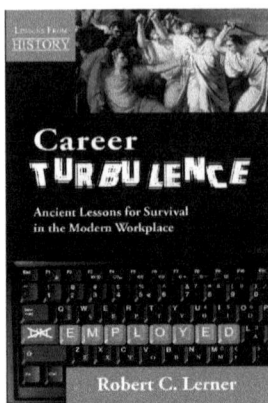

Career Turbulence: Ancient Lessons for Survival in the Modern Workplace

The loss of a job can result in the complete destruction of your personal wealth. In unsettled economic times, remaining employed is even more critical because a lost job may be impossible to replace. In such periods, a different set of rules needs to be followed—rules far more Darwinian than in normal times.

Author Robert Lerner examines the decisions and actions of an ancient Roman businessman named Titus Pomponius Atticus, who lived in the cut-throat world of Julius Caesar, Mark Antony, Marcus Brutus, and Cicero. Atticus was a sophisticated financier who did business with these giants of history, witnessed their rise and fall, and endured the years of civil war they engendered. Atticus was a survivor who knew how to manoeuvre through the political traps and intrigues of this dangerous world. From Atticus' ancient decisions and actions, Lerner has developed 20 lessons that can be applied to situations found in today's workplace.

The goal of this book is to help readers better prepare for periods of career turbulence and survive in the modern jungle we call "the marketplace."

ISBN-13:   9781554891702   (paperback)

Available in print and electronic formats.

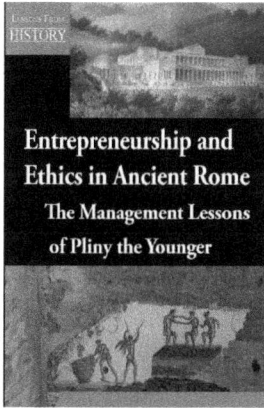

Entrepreneurship and Ethics in Ancient Rome: The Management Lessons of Pliny the Younger

It was fall and the late summer rains had produced an overly-abundant grape harvest. Such a large harvest was driving down grape prices. Brokers who bought grape futures at premium prices early in the summer would be selling at a tremendous loss. The largest growers faced a dilemma: hold brokers to their contracts, causing longer-term disruption in the futures market; or renegotiate supply contracts to ease the financial burden on the brokers, ensuring a stable marketplace and building customer loyalty.

What may surprise you is that this challenging scenario ocurred 1,900 years ago during the Roman Empire. Many of our modern business problems were confronted then – and resolved – without the aid of modern technologies.

This book reveals how one ancient entrepreneur overcame this challenge to maintain customer loyalty, manage his sales channel, motivate people, resolve conflicts and ethical dilemmas, and more. The book reveals lessons learned that can be applied to today's business environment.

ISBN-13:   9781554891313   (paperback)

Available in print and electronic formats.

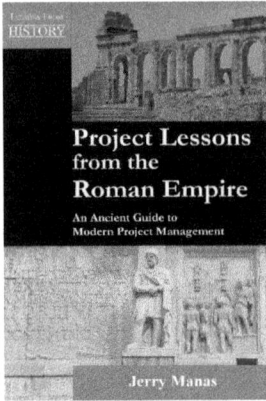

Project Lessons from the Roman Empire: An Ancient Guide to Modern Project Management

The leaders of the Roman Empire established many of the organizational governance practices that we follow today, in addition to remarkable feats of engineering using primitive tools that produced roads and bridges which are still being used today, complex irrigation systems, and even "flush toilets." Yet, the leaders were challenged with political intrigue, rebelling team members, and pressure from the competition. How could they achieve such long-lasting greatness in the face of these challenges?

In this new addition to the Lessons from History series, join author Jerry Manas as he takes you on a journey through history to learn about project management the Roman way. Discover the 23 key lessons that can be learned from the successes and failures of the Roman leadership, with specific advice on how they can be applied to today's projects.

Read this intriguing book to learn how they did it.

ISBN-13:   9781554890545   (paperback)

Available in print and electronic formats. Order directly from the publisher at **www.mmpubs.com**.

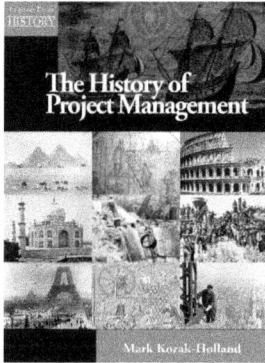

The History of Project Management

The Pyramid of Giza, the Colosseum, and the Transcontinental Railroad are all great historical projects from the past four millennia. When we look back, we tend to look at these as great architectural or engineering works. Project management tends to be overlooked, and yet its core principles were used extensively in these projects.

Mark Kozak-Holland explores the history of project management and how it evolved over the past 4,500 years. This book shows that "modern" project management practices did not just appear in the past 100 years but have been used — often with a lot of sophistication — for thousands of years.

As readers explore the many case studies in this book, they will discover fascinating details of innovative projects that produced many of our most famous landmarks and voyages of discovery.

ISBN-13:   9781554890965   (Hardcover)

Available in print and electronic formats. Order directly from the publisher at **www.mmpubs.com**.

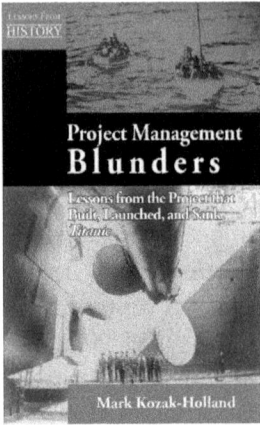

Project Management Blunders: Lessons from the Project that Built, Launched, and Sank Titanic

White Star's initiative to build its new Olympic-class ships can be described as a text book project. It started off very well in the initiation and planning phases: the project team had a very good understanding of the business and customer needs, a solid vision, a superlative business case, the right supplier partnerships, good stakeholder relationships, and a healthy balance of proven and emerging technologies.

By the end of the design phase, however, decisions were made that compromised safety features. By the end of the fitting-out phase, all key stakeholders believed that the ships could never founder.

Mark Kozak-Holland reveals the project management blunders that doomed *Titanic* while it was still being built. Filled with photos and copies of actual documents from the project, this book walks you through a case study in project management failure.

ISBN-13:   9781554891221   (paperback)

Available in print and electronic formats. Order directly from the publisher at **www.mmpubs.com**.

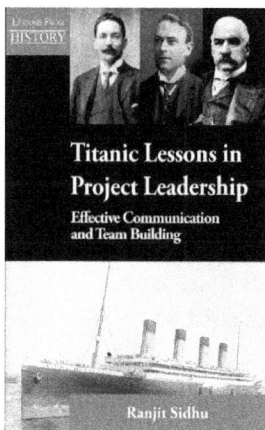

Titanic Lessons in
Project Leadership

Effective Communication
and Team Building

Ranjit Sidhu

Titanic Lessons in Project Leadership: Effective Communication and Team Building

In *Titanic Lessons in Project Leadership* we see how "small" and easily overlooked behavioral and communication issues can aggregate through a project to become seemingly unthinkable errors.

This book focuses on the people aspects of the *Titanic* story; the key stakeholders, power dynamics, underlying perceptions, communication, leadership and team interactions. Ranjit Sidhu draws on this tragic tale to focus on the "behind the scenes" aspects of human communication and leadership to guide you in the right direction for making that vital difference to your current projects.

Combining contemporary management theory with her own insights and extensive project management experience, Ranjit offers practical guidance and lessons from history that will help you gain a deeper understanding of how leaders and teams can operate at their very best.

ISBN-13:   9781554891207   (paperback)

Available in print and electronic formats. Order directly from the publisher at **www.mmpubs.com**.

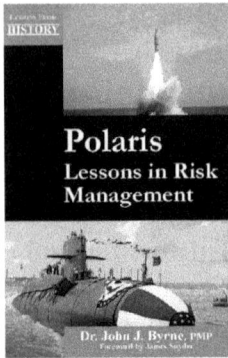

Polaris: Lessons in Risk Management

Risk management is one of the most important practices that a manager can employ to help drive a successful outcome from a project. Good risk management allows organizations to proactively respond to risks.

Unfortunately, many managers believe risk management to be too time consuming or too complicated. Some find it to be shrouded in mystery.

This book by Dr. John J. Byrne, PMP is designed to demystify risk management, explaining introductory and advanced risk management approaches in simple language. This book uses real-life examples from a very influential project that helped change the course of world history -- the project that designed and built the *Polaris* missile and accompanying submarine launch system that became a key deterrent to a Soviet nuclear attack during the Cold War.

Containing a foreword by James R. Snyder, one of the founders of the Project Management Institute (PMI), this book is structured to align with the risk management approach described in PMI's the *Project Management Body of Knowledge (PMBOK Guide)*.

ISBN-13:   9781554890972 (Paperback)

Available in print and electronic formats. Order directly from the publisher at **www.mmpubs.com**.

Agile Leadership and the Management of Change: Project Lessons from Winston Churchill and the Battle of Britain

Around the turn of the millennium, there was a poll conducted in Britain that asked who people thought was the most influential person in all of Britain's history. The winner: Winston Churchill. What set Churchill above the others was his leadership qualities: his ability to create and share a powerful vision, his ability to motivate the population in the face of tremendous fear, and his ability to get others to rally behind him and quickly turn his visions into reality. By any measure, Winston Churchill was a powerful leader.

What many don't know, however, was how Churchill used his leadership skills to restructure the British military, government, and even the British manufacturing sector to support his efforts to rearm the country and get ready for an imminent enemy invasion in early 1940.

Join author Mark Kozak-Holland as he explores how Churchill acted as the head project manager of a massive change project that affected the daily lives of millions of people. Learn about Churchill's change management and agile management techniques and how they can be applied to today's projects.

ISBN-13:   9781554890354   (Paperback)

Available in print and electronic formats. Order directly from the publisher at **www.mmpubs.com**.